PROFILE
of an
ICONOCLAST

ABNE M. EISENBERG

For further information about this book,
contact: Abné M. Eisenberg, Ph.D.,
100 Bluff View Drive, Suite 515-C Belleaire Bluffs, Florida 33770,
email address: aeisenberg3@tampabay.rr.com

Trafford rev. 09/24/2015

www.trafford.com
North America & international
toll-free: 1 888 232 4444 (USA & Canada)
fax: 812 355 4082

DEDICATION

———⟨⟨◈⟩⟩———

To Marianna, my dearest wife who made me complete.

ACKNOWLEDGEMENT

Ed Stevens has blessed me with the kind of
friendship I thought no longer existed.

CONTENTS

WELCOME

⸻ ⸰❰◉❱⸰ ⸻

These essays were created in the 90th year of my life. They consist of current as well as recurrent thoughts about a variety of things. They range from the rational to the irrational, logical to the illogical, practical to the impractical, serious to the frivolous.

Hopefully, this work will amaze and amuse the itinerant reader. In my sixty year tenure as a university professor of communication, I have tried to make students think – to think about things differently.

The content of the pages that lie ahead constitute my pre-mortem eulogy. While all my physical remains will suffer the ravages of time, my hope is that my words will endure.

My philosophy of life is three-fold:

Maximize compliments, minimize criticism.

Ideas have consequences

Everything is a matter of definition.

AME

LYING TO YOURSELF

T here may come a time when virtual reality will enable you to see yourself as you really are and how you are perceived by others. The image you now have of yourself is a fabrication, an illusion, a wishful dream.

College students were once required to perform an interesting exercise in a communication class. Their professor asked them to answer this question ten times: "Who are you"? Most of them listed their first response by writing, "I am John or Mary." or "I am a student" They, then, had to come up with nine more answers. Some had difficulty coming up with ten separate and distinct answers. A few repeated an answer several times.

There are many people who do not want to know what they are really like. If someone at a party raised a glass to propose a toast by saying, "May we all get what we deserve," some would say yes, others would say no. Such a toast is often taken to be ill- mannered and socially intrusive.

Self-deception is a safety net, a security blanket. There are those who prefer living an "as if" life. There are smart people who think they are not smart, beautiful people who think they are ugly, dishonest people who fancy themselves honest, lazy people who insist they are motivated. These individuals are living a counterfeit identity.

The lies we tell ourselves lead us astray. If we created them, we can uncreate them. We all have within us a beautiful SELF patiently waiting to be born. Reality is an unrelentless opponent. Conquering it requires a heaping dose of self-determination. Shakespere captured its essence with these two maxims, "To be or not to be, that is the question." And, "To thine own self be true."

Tomorrow look into a mirror and say, "I am a very special person. I like who I am and will continue to invest my life with self-respect, self-worth, and self- confidence. I will stop lying to myself."

LIVING IN A BLAND WORLD

---««◎»»---

T he word <u>bland</u> is most commonly used to describe a diet that avoids extremes in taste and digestibility. Here, it is metaphorically used to describe a life that takes a middle road which minimizes risk and lacks passion and imagination.

What would it be like living in a world without heretics, iconoclasts, rebels, or revolutionaries? Would it be dull, dreary, and monotonous? Despite this bleak portrait, many people might find such a bland and blissful existence the ultimate in peace and happiness. Dreamers imagine that it would be like what James Hilton described in his book, <u>Shangri-La</u>.

In an informal study, several people were asked, "What if you could create your own Utopia. How would it look?, Here are some of the features they said should be included: Complete religious freedom, no pollution, mutual respect, animals would be free, no wars, no crime, no governmental control, no disease, perfect weather all the time, a universal language, free housing, lots of parks with beautiful flowers.

Living life in the fictitious Shangri-La, or in the Utopia Aldous Huxley describes in his book, the <u>Brave New World</u>, is only for dreamers. Reality tells a different story. Some examples of mankind's greatest achievements include the Colosseum of Rome, Pyramids of Egypt, Great wall of China., Michu Pichu, Panama Canal, Taj Mahal, and the international Space Station. If these magnificent accomplishments are contrasted with civilization's most horrific events such as the Crusades, Inquisition, bubonic plague, holocaust in WW II, and the dropping of the Atomic bomb, the notion of a <u>bland</u> society becomes absurd.

If reality is put aside, living in a bland society only exists in the mind of fiction writers and film makers who take their viewers into a world of virtual reality. Whatever the context, <u>bland</u> is boring.

ON THE OUTSKIRTS OF SANITY

T hree people live inside us: who we were, who we are, and who we will become. Our sanity depends upon how each of these identities manage our perception of reality.

Throughout history, sanity has been described differently. While some of its characteristics are universal, differences have affected attitudes, values, and beliefs. For example, primitive cultures turned to (and still do) witch doctors or shamans who employ magic, herbal mixtures, or chanting to rid deranged individuals of evil spirits or bizarre behavior. Archeologists have recovered skulls 7,000 year old with holes in them used to allow demons to escape. The practice was called trephining.

During the 18th century, the French and British began treating the insane more humanely. While the infamous hospital in London called Bedlam did employ certain medical criteria to determine a patient's admission, their treatment was outrageously cruel. They conducted paid tours for the public to observe insane people like caged animals.

Today, in spite of the benefits that modern medicine has provided for the mentally ill, it continues to see only one side of the picture. In Thomas Szasz's book, "The Myth of Mental Illness" he questioned the legitimacy of his field and made enemies of many fellow doctors. His book hammered away at the discipline likening it to alchemy and astrology."

In the 1975 film, "One Flew Over the Cuckoo's Nest," viewers witnessed the unconscionable use of electroshock treatment and lobotomies. The practice was reminiscent of the trephining mentioned earlier.

Here we are, in the 21st century, flying around in outer space, transplanting hearts, cloning sheep, using the Internet to download the entire Library of Congress and genetically discovering the role played by our of DNA and RNA. Despite these incredulous technologic advances, much of our mental health remains a mystery. Psychiatric theories raise more questions than they answer.

No matter how hard neuroscientists have tried to categorize insanity, it has only revealed brief glimpses into its complex nature,. A mind-reading machine has yet to be invented. An EEG measures electricity that the brain makes; it does NOT measure thoughts or feelings, There is one thing in which researchers have great confidence; that the unconscious or subconscious mind play a critical role in the maintenance of our sanity.

It has taken years for the scientific community to accept psychology as a science. If Copernicus, Darwin, or Einstein had been faithful to the strict scientific method, they would never have published their theories and would have been bogged down in the outskirts of scientific discovery.

SPARE THE ROD, SPOIL THE CHILD

"If we are ever to turn toward
a kindlier society and a safer
world, a revulsion against the
physical punishment of children
children would be a good place
to start.."

Benjamin Spock, *M.D.*

The debate concerning the validity of this proverb has been going on for centuries. Those who abide by it have prevailed the longest. Now, the tide has shifted in favor of permissiveness. Today, parent abhor spanking or physically disciplining their children. On television, we see children, especially teenagers, disrespecting their parents with impunity.

This practice infuriates most seniors citizens. They insist that appropriately spanking an unruly child builds character. It teaches that certain forms of behavior are wrong and warrant being addressed by responsible parents.

Kimberly Sirl, a clinical psychologist at St. Louis Children's Hospital argues that "Spanking doesn't work. It just makes kids mistrustful and aggressive. What we're teaching them is fear, rather than responsibility and problem-solving."

In any form of responsible child-rearing, a balance must be struck between the seriousness of a child's misbehavior and the severity of the discipline administered.

The American Academy of Pediatrics opposes spanking because research shows it results in long-term aggression in children. The more children are spanked, the more anger they exhibit as adults, the more likely they are to spank their own children.

When it comes to how a naughty child should be punished, the word "appropriate" invariably arises. A great deal depends upon how the word is culturally defined. In some countries, disciplining a child goes far beyond a loving slap on a child's bottom. In the last five years, still only 5.2% of the world's children live where they are protected in law from assault in the guise of "discipline"

While there is a current global movement to protect the rights of children, a significant number of parents continue to condone the axiom. "Spare the rod and spoil the child." Trying to calmly explain to a five year old why he/she shouldn't do something is an exercise in futility. A gentle smack on the buttock usual does more good than the words of a caring and responsible parent.

Every parent, past and present, should take the time to investigate the pros and cons of the issue being raised here.

WHAT MAKES YOU TICK?

A side from being a collection of anatomical body parts that differentiate you from every other person on Earth, there are invisible forces that make you tick; i.e., your attitudes, values, and beliefs. Unlike removing your appendix, a surgeon cannot remove a questionable attitude or belief.

Although your thoughts and the air you breath are invisible, they influence the quality of your life. One morning, you desire pancakes for breakfast or just a slice of toast and coffee. That afternoon, you get a phone call saying that a good friend was taken to the hospital. Both events cause you to behave and feel differently.

There are inner-directed and other-directed people. The former behave according to what they think and feel. The latter, according to how other people behave in a given situation. Inner-directed types embrace what has also been referred to as the Galatea Effect, other-directed types, the Pygmalion Effect.

Your entire inner and outer self is unique. If you are an extrovert, friends and family are usually able to anticipate how you would react in a particular situation.. If you are an introvert, a shy and private individual, people will usually have difficulty predicting your behavior.

While stereotyping is something to be discouraged, it often contains an element of truth. Most people have a good or bad reputation in their neighborhood. The rare few are reclusive and often referred to as hermits.

Social scientists have studied the behavior of ordinary people around the world. Their research determined that, while certain behavioral traits were universal, many were indigenous to particular groups. What interested them most was the mind-set of famous people. What made Socrates, Leonardo Da Vinci, Michelangelo, Galileo. Shakespere, Pasteur, and Einstein tick? Did their brain contain some unusual neurological feature or did they possess an atypical gene?

In an effort to better understand human behavior, experts in animal behavior have made great strides by monitoring the behavior of various creatures They paid special attention to our closest evolutionary relatives, gorillas, chimpanzees, and orangutans. Their most intriguing discovery dealt with their means of survival. They only killed in self-defense or for food. While the Neanderthal also killed for food and in self-defense, modern humans went one step further, they killed for fun and an ideology.

In addition to historical genocide, Adolph Hitler's nefarious ideology in WW II resulted in the extermination of millions of Jews and other less fortunate individuals. Did only his warped ideology make him tick?

On almost a regular basis, today's media cites individuals who suddenly go on killing spree. Psychiatrists are hired to find out what made them tick. In a courtroom, rival theories challenge juries.

Sigmund Freud's efforts to better understand human behavior centered upon his conception of a conscious and unconscious mind. He invested these areas with what he called the ego, superego, Id, and libido. He theorized that these attributes dictated what makes us tick. Psychoanalyst Carl Jung believed that we all possess a deep layer of the mind he called archetypes, propensities causing us to respond to certain universal themes.

A further notion of what makes us tick was advanced by psychologist Abraham Maslow. He suggested five basic needs: physiological (food and air), safety (shelter) love & belonging (emotional gratification, connectedness), esteem (positive self-worth and self-image), and self-actualization (becoming the best that you can, achieving your highest level of fulfillment). He later added self-transcendence (service to others).

We have long left behind the grunts and groans of our Neanderthal ancestors and are still grappling with what makes us tick. While there are many theories, there are few credible answers. Ask yourself, "What makes me tick?" You will quickly appreciate the paradox.

IS CURSIVE WRITING DEAD?

S ince Johannes Guttenberg invented the printing press in 1436, handwriting has experienced an ongoing struggle to stay alive. Current technology has put cursive writing in the ICU of communication. Fewer and fewer schools are teaching it and, in the very near future, it will have joined the dinosaurs in extinction.

For decades, we tapped away on our typewriters, reproduced copy on a mimeograph machine, and wrote with white chalk on classroom blackboards. Homework reports were either handwritten or typed. Handwritten notes left on refrigerator doors, shopping lists, and memos scribbled on calendars are all rapidly disappearing.

In the US, schoolchildren traditionally learned cursive writing from about eight years of age, but with the introduction of the Common Core State Standards Initiative back in 2010, as many as 45 states opted out of teaching cursive writing.

While email and texted messages today are quicker and more expeditious, they fail to communicate the same kind of gratitude that a handwritten thank you card conveys. Similarly, a handwritten letter from a son or daughter in the military delivers a great deal more heartfelt sentiment than an email or a cell phone call.

The most persuasive argument advocating the abolition of writing in longhand is the element of time. If all of today's communication had to be done by hand, there would not be enough hours in the day.

Ironically, there are still employers who require that employment applications be handwritten. The Chartered Institute of Personnel and Development warns that making such a requirement could invite charges of discrimination.

Another symptom of handwriting's death is the disappearance of ink-filled fountain pens. Only those hooked on nostalgia, who treasure a poem penned by the poet or an original document handwritten by one of our founding fathers, still use fountain pens.

If we continue on our technologically expanding means of communicating, the lost art of handwriting will eventually be reduced to only the signing of our name.

Once the upcoming generation is no longer able to read cursive writing, it will be completely divorced from all the famous documents written is script unless they are re-written in a contemporary readable format.

Fortunately, all may not be lost. Recently, the state legislators of Tennessee, Florida, Kansas, North Carolina, Utah, Georgia, Arkansas and Idaho have mandated the inclusion of cursive writing into the curricula of their schools. California, Indiana, Hawaii and Massachusetts are also considering such legislation. Interestingly, it never occurred to Roman Catholic school administers to eliminate cursive writing from their curriculum.

They feel that a competence in cursive writing contributes to a student's reading, writing, language development and critical thinking skills. Teresa McKay teaches fifth and sixth graders at St. Mary School in Paragould, As. . She contends, "If you go back in history, all of the original historical documents are written cursively. Eventually no one will be able to read historical documents if cursive writing isn't taught."

It is highly unlikely that the handwriting controversy will be resolved in the immediate future. Traditional handwriting has too long an established history to be arbitraily dismissed.

THE BRAIN CAN BE A GARBAGE BIN

E very sound or image to which our brain is exposed is forever stored as short or long term memory. Learning how to drive a car initially involves short term memory where one must quickly remember what a driving instructor has just said. Long term memory involves the ability to recall that information for future years of driving.

For storage purposes, the brain must make a distinction between information that is relevant or irrelevant, superficial or profound, and its degree of intensity.

Since the biochemical agents the brain needs to facilitate retrievable information changes over the years, memory lapses reflect these changes.

Recent brain research has discovered that the brain has the ability to inhibit or enhance pleasant and unpleasant memories. While this ability has had only limited clinical trials, its potential is encouraging. Once its effectiveness has been therapeutically established, it may be helpful in the treatment of Alzheimer's, Parkinson, and amnesia.

Likening the brain to a garbage bin makes the word "clutter" very significant. Its like trying to find something is a room containing a great many unrelated objects. The things we arbitrarily throw into a garbage bin is also cluttered.

Not unlike a computer, normal thinking requires that the brain sort through all the stored mental garbage until it finds the neural connections that comport with a desired idea or thought.

Remedial courses in critical thinking can help an individual better cope with brain garbage by refining the ability to focus. Meditation helps the brain focus more effectively.

The senses of an autistic individual are not compromised. They see, hear, taste, touch, and smell the way normal people do. Their problem involves an inability to appropriately process information. Their perception and conception of things is abnormal. As a result, they get hung up on brain garbage, constantly repeating a meaningless phrase or exhibit some form of senseless repetitive muscular behavior.

Under hypnosis or in regressive therapy, the brain is capable of tapping into a stockpile of mental garbage stored into the subconscious mind; e.g., words, names, places, or situations.

How much of the garbage stored in the brain is actually needed to live a full and rewarding life? A majority of it has no immediate purpose or relevance. The brain must constantly conduct a filtering process; garbage in, garbage out. Will Rogers reminded us, "It isn't what we don't know that gives us trouble, it's what we know that ain't so."

The amount of garbage spewed out by the media on television, in newspapers, and on the Internet has converted average citizens into inadvertent garbage collectors. Our brains have become a virtual garbage bin. We are defenseless against offensive incoming thoughts. Any effort to consciously re-direct or re-focus our attention invariably fails. Unwanted thoughts are stubborn residents of the miind

To reduce the amount of garbage the brain collects, scientists have uncovered something called the glymphatic system that works best during sleep. How this system works, however, needs additional research.

The point being made here is that brain garbage can be an asset or a liability. In certain religions, especially Hinduism, an effort is made to clear the mind, to erase all conscious thoughts. Perhaps a better approach would be to learn how to effectively manage the garbage and, by so doing, strengthen one's self-image and one's self-control.

HINDSIGHT, FORESIGHT, INSIGHT

A wareness has three faces, looking back, looking forward, and looking inward. Although looking back is the easiest, it can be somewhat sketchy. Looking into the future is more difficult. Looking into ourselves is the most difficult. Each of these perspectives can reveal a segment of an individual's life.

We all search for a path to follow, one that will give us the greatest amount of satisfaction. Unfortunately, most people go to their grave wondering whether they had chosen the right path.

Psychiatrist Kurt Goldstein considered something he labeled self-actualization, the achievement of one's full potential. He observed that most people experience only an approximation of that potential.

Psychoanalytic couches groan with people trying to better understand why they think and act a certain way. With the analyst as their guide, they explore the past (hindsight). The information it reveals often provides a glimpse into a patient's mind-set (insight) Hopefully, this will propose an appropriate form of future treatment(foresight).

An axiom by Bill Kean provides us with a unique view of how we perceive civilization. "Yesterday is history, tomorrow is a mystery, today is a gift, which is why we call it the present."

While most people are curious to know what makes them tick, others are comfortable with the unknown. They avoid fortune-tellers, soothsayers, clairvoyants, and palm-readers. They rely upon fate, kismet, and karma to dictate their destiny.

Again, when people talk to themselves out loud or in silence, it is called intrapersonal communication. This internal conversation can be constructive or destructive, calming or unsettling. enlightening or confusing.

TRUST IS A MUST

People who believe everything they see or hear have been called "intellectual virgins." Most of us calibrate our trust. We believe a doctor more than a perfect stranger. We take care that what we are told doesn't clash with our previous beliefs. Vladimir Lenin and Ronald Reagan were fond of saying, ""Trust, but verify."

At an early age, children are inclined to believe everything they are told by an adult.. They lack the life experience enabling them to understand why someone should or should not be trusted.

Trust has been defined as, "The reliance on the integrity, ability, or character of a person or thing." Our entire life is based upon trust. Try and think of something that does not, directly or indirectly, depend upon trust.

Throughout history, every recorded event involved a measure of trust. Religions depend upon the unconditional trust of their followers. When someone is asked the familiar question, "Do you believe in God?" how they respond reflects their unconditional trust that God exists. During the Spanish Inquisition, a failure to have that trust often resulted in death or torture.

During the McCarthy hearings in fifties, Americans were required to declare their trust and faith in our system of government. In an effort to weed out communists, the committee demanded that those brought before it prove that they had an unabiding trust in America. A refusal to comply with the committee's demands often caused the person to be blacklisted and denied an opportunity to earn a living in their chosen profession.

The Nuremberg Trial after WW II also involved trust. Could the appointed judges for this tribunal be trusted? Could the testimony rendered by Nazi's on trial be trusted?

In every country, citizens are expected to trust their leaders. Regardless of whether their government is democratic or autocratic, trust is always the *sine qua non* -something that is indispensible.

Trust always has a consequence. If you purchase a new car, you trust that it will operate properly. When you dine out in an expensive restaurant, you trust that certain health laws are obeyed in the kitchen. Every medication taken is accompanied by a trust that it will do what it says on the bottle.

An occasional betrayal of one's trust is usually well tolerated. However, when it occurs repeatedly, that trust gets weaker. When a climate of distrust afflicts a nation, its impact creates a variety of symptoms. When it reaches a tipping point, feelings such as alienation, helplessness, detachment and indifference soon become a societal malignancy.

Perhaps we should rethink our expectations of a civilized world. Rather than making fruitless attempts to curb all the distrust, we should seek ways of constructively adapting to it.

Punishing those who betray our trust has not worked. It has, in fact, inspired them to invent more effective ways of betraying that trust.

The United States was once among the most trusted nations in the world. That distinction has since suffered a serious decline. People no longer trust their neighbors as well as their government. 9We are definitely on a slippery slope. Optimism is rapidly giving way to pessimism.

The Internet is based upon trust. What would happen if every transaction could be viciously manipulated by anyone so inclined; i.e., when we no longer know who is who and what is what? Do we have to rethink our dependence on personal information for authentication knowing full-well that data is easily accessible and not really a secret? Has technologic advances created a monster we can no longer control?

A great many people suffer at least one hurtful betrayal of their trust in a lifetime. When that happens, it should not completely their sense of trust in the future.

TRANSCEND YOUR MORTALITY

P hilosophers suggest that only humans have a sense of their own mortality. Perhaps it is better to think of how you live, rather than how long you live.

For most people, satisfaction usually focuses on family, career, and having good health. longevity continues to be an enigma..

Think of mortality as a bank account with a credit and debit sheet. Is it an interest-bearing account that delivers a predictable a bonus? In mortal terms, that bonus comes in the form of fond memories.

Sophisticated drugs and incredible surgical advances have enabled people to live longer than they did a century ago. Career-changes at age forty or fifty are not uncommon. Adult education has encouraged countless senior citizens to go back to school. The increase in leisure time has become big business. If our longevity continues to lengthen, it will challenge how we manage things such as health care, social security, and housing.

If you were offered immortality, would you accept it? Most people would not because those they loved would be dead. Those who would jump at the chance seem untroubled by the thought of leaving behind their loved ones. They boast that they would simply start another life.

A memorable film that addressed immortality was titled, "The Picture of Dorian Gray" written by Oscar Wilde. In it, a young man named Dorian Gray has a painting of himself in his attic that spares him the ravages of aging. He remains young and the painting ages.

Plastic surgery is the most prevalent hedge against the ravages of aging. Almost every part of the body can be cosmetically altered.

However, unless the procedure is a medical necessity, it is not covered by health insurance.

Our pre-occupation with mortality goes back to the fictional Methuselah, a descendent of Adam, who lived for 969 years. Obviously, the author of this myth had a different conception of time.

How should the qualities of a life be measured? Should a yardstick include wealth, property, progeny, education, intelligence, character, reputation, altruism, or creativity? Once people die, the quality and character of their life dies with them. All that remains are their accomplishments.

Historically, there were always individuals who had an irresistible desire to make a difference, to initiate change, to matter. The majority have lived routine lives in which they ate, slept, worked, and made babies.

In many cultures, death is not conceived as an end, but a new beginning. In Judeo-Christian religions, it is called the afterlife. The deceased ascend to a variety of places called Heaven, Paradise, Nirvana, Happy Hunting Ground, and the Elysian Fields.

When it comes to death and dying, hope is essential. People have a thirst for something beyond life as they know it. If a leap of faith is needed, it should be courageously taken. In David Carr's book, The Night of the Gun, he factiously challenges our mortality with, "I now inhabit a life I don't deserve, but we all walk this earth feeling we are frauds. The trick is to be grateful and hope the caper doesn't end any time soon"

ARE WE SHEEP OR SHEPHERDS?

‒‒‒‒‒‒‒◉‒‒‒‒‒‒‒

Sheep are creatures of habit. They do what all the other sheep are doing. Shepherds attend the sheep by regulating where they graze, protect them from predators, tag them for identification, keep them from eating poisonous plants, examine them for signs of illness, administers vaccines, medications, and insecticides, and assists in lambing, docking, and shearing.

Like sheep, the over 7 billion people on Earth do pretty much the same thing. They eat, sleep, work, and make babies.

But why are people equated with sheep? In Psalm 100.3, it reads, "Know that Yahweh, he is God. It is he who has made us, and we are his. We are his people, and the sheep of his pasture." Millions identify themselves with this biblical reference to sheep.

Separating themselves from this majority is a smaller group of people who identify themselves as shepherds. They consist of government and locally elected officials who enforce various rules and regulations.

It is important that the sheep analogy not be taken to mean that ordinary people are ignorant or stupid. What is being suggested is that there is such a thing as a group-mind or group-thinking. Both people and sheep are motivated by an innate tendency to conform -- to act in concert with other members of their specie.

Shepherds are leaders, rather than followers. While there is a residual element of conformism among shepherds, it is not their primary source of motivation.

People resent being labeled. While clerics are comfortable being labeled a shepherd of their flock, politicians are not that comfortable with the allegation.

Stereotyping, in any form, has always been considered an insulting form of communication. Nevertheless, it continues to be a common public practice.

The saying, "Sticks and stones will brake your bones, but names will never harm you." is not true. If someone is accused of being a child molester and is subsequently proven to be innocent, parents still tend to keep their children away from the individual.

Few people will look in a mirror and admit that a sheep or a shepherd is looking back at them. People see what they want to see. Shakespere wrote, "To thine own self be true." There is no meaning in words, only in people. Labels should only be used to identify, differentiate, or classify objects, --- not people.

HOW SEREDIPITY CAN
CHANGE YOUR LIFE

Serendipity is when a completely unexpected event occurs. Imagine a woman who suffers from migraine headaches. She has consulted several physicians without success. One day, at a neighbor's Christmas party, she is introduced to a distinguish gentleman who also complained of migraine headaches. During the conversation, he raved about a physician in Baton Rouge, Louisiana, that cured him. Impressed by this news, she decides to fly there and see this doctor. The end result is that her migraines disappeared.

Whether this anecdote is true or not is unimportant. What is important is that, had she not gone to that Christmas party, she would not have met that man and still be suffering from migraines.

A great many people experience similar events, but fail to take them seriously. They write them off as coincidence, chance, or happenstance.

Serendipitous events are meaningless unless they are perceived as windows of opportunity. They are forks in the road that invite making a choice. The word "disappointment" is not in the vocabulary of someone who believes in serendipity.

Another case of serendipity involved the discovery of penicillin. When Scottish researcher, Sir Alexander Fleming, returned to his lab from a vacation, he noticed that a mold had formed on an accidentally contaminated staphylococcus culture dish. Instead of simply tossing it into a waste paper basket, he noticed that the mold prevented the growth of the staphylococci bacteria. Without his inquisitive nature, we would never have had the curative benefits of penicillin.

Another term consonant with serendipity is synchronicity. It occurs when two completely unrelated events compliment one another. A woman buys a red dress at a local department store and, by mistake, she is sent a black dress. The next day, she gets a call from Florida saying that her grandmother had passed away. The black dress now becomes appropriate for her grandmother's funeral, but did not cause her death.

Studies of serendipity found that people who react assertively to unexpected events have more self-confidence and are more open-minded. They have a more relaxed approach to life, worry less about details, and think outside the box.

Most people are victims of routine. Their lives consist of a highly predictable series of daily events. Any deviation from their daily routine makes them feel uncomfortable.

Serendipitous language includes phrases like, "Isn't that interesting?" "I'd like to give it a try," and "Nothing ventured, nothing gained."

Developing a healthy attitude toward serendipity requires doing things differently. Open doors with your left hand, get into bed from the other side, compliment the next person you meet."

Any change in your routine produces neurological changes in your brain. Even though some serendipitous opportunities are not acted jupon, others are always on the horizon. If nothing else is learned from making changes, it is that serendipity is a portal of entry to a more joyful and fulfilling life.

FROM GRUNTS TO GRAMMAR

I n Genesis of the Old Testament, we find the prophetic phrase, *"In the beginning was the word."* It set the stage for the origin of language. Mounting that evolutionary stage attracted a wide variety of theories. While each theory touched upon some aspect of how language evolved, five theories attracted the most attention. They included the <u>Bow-Wow Theory</u> which suggested that language derived from imitating the sounds made by animals, the <u>Ding-Dong Theory</u>, a response to sounds generated by the environment, the <u>La-La Theory</u> -- emotion-sensitive sounds reflecting how people felt, the <u>Pooh-Pooh Theory</u> -- spontaneous cries of pain (Ouch!) and surprise (Oh!). Finally, the <u>Yo-He-Ho Theory</u> -- the grunts, groans, and snorts people make when doing heavy physical labor.

The origin of language has plagued scholars for centuries. Because no direct evidence is available, they have had to resort to inferences by fossil records, primate communication, and archaeological artifacts. Because of the controversy, the Linguistic Society of Paris in 1866 banned any existing or future debates on the subject. Today, 150 years later, there continues to be a lack of consensus among linguists.

Imagine what would happen if, suddenly, we were deprived of language. All we would be able to do is make the guttural sounds of our cave-dwelling ancestors. Everything that our superior linguistic ability made possible no longer existed. No telephone, electricity, computers, film, flight, literature, medicine, and host of others things that involve language All that we now take for granted can be traced to the acquisition and evolution of language.

How would personal relationships fare without the current nature of our language? Aside from being able to share interpersonal communication on a most primitive level, it is our ability to move into that invisible world of abstraction such as love, courage, loyalty, and compassion that makes us different. Language enables us to conceptualize people, places, and things that do not materially exist; i.e., heaven, hell, extra-terrestrials, Santa Claus, and the existence of a soul or ego. We are the only creatures on the planet that possess that ability.

While grunts and groans do continue to have primal meaning, Darwinian thinking has promoted us to the head of the class. It will now be interesting to see how we honor that distinction in the future.

IGNORANT DOESN'T MEAN STUPID

B eing ignorant is simply not knowing, being stupid is a lack of intelligence and an inability to understand or reason. Stupidity should be pitied because it is something an individual cannot help. Ignorance is more complicated. It may result from a lack of motivation, inadequate education, or the social climate in which a person is reared. In both ignorance and stupidity, the degree is important.

In the award winning film, "Forrest Gump," Tom Hank's character is aware that he is not too swift. Actually, those with a marginal I.Q. are generally aware of their psychological inadequacy. This is not so with most people who are ignorant. Ignorant people often rationalize their lack of knowledge or awareness.

Pretending to be ignorant is a ploy certain people deliberately use to gain a social advantage. In addition, ignorant people have been known to do stupid things and stupid people to do intelligent things.

Paradoxically, some stupid people possess a variety of skills. An example is the "Savant" who is retarded in all other ways, but demonstrates an extraordinary proficiency in areas such as mathematics, music, or art.

A clear distinction between stupidity and ignorance remains an enigma. Here are thoughts advanced by two notable figures:

"To be conscious that you are ignorant is a great step to knowledge. "(Benjamin Disraeli) "Only two things are infinite, the universe and stupidity, and I am not sure about the former." (Albert Einstein)"

Although these quotations do little to help us understand the difference between ignorance and stupidity, they prompt us to reflect upon the role that each plays in a world lacking the wisdom to learn from its prior experience. Too often, the mistakes we make derive from our ignorance or stupidity.

IS PREACHING AND TEACHING THE SAME?

A ccording to Pastor Greg S. Baker, "Preaching is trying to affect a person's thinking by appealing to a person's heart. Teaching is trying to affect a person's heart by appealing to their thinking." Another distinction between preaching and teaching is that preaching is uni-directional, whereas teaching is multi-directional. Most people are not aware of the importance or distinction between these two ways of communicating.

In current public schools and colleges, educators are admonished for preaching, rather than teaching. For some reason, preaching in a classroom has a negative connotation; i.e., "Don't preach to me, teach me."

Teaching and preaching in the New Testament are inseparable. In the New Testament, teaching was to explain ideas and their implications. and preaching to announce the good news centered around the themes espoused by Jesus. Paul reflected the interchangeability between preaching and teaching when he said, "Him we preach, warning every man and teaching every man in all wisdom, that we may present every man perfect in Him we preach in Jesus Christ."

It appears that teaching and preaching in the earliest Christian communities were the same activities and had the same content in many instances.

While varying degrees of passion exist in both preaching and teaching, it is more pronounced in preaching. Classroom teaching is traditionally more didactic than dramatic. Put simply, preaching emphasizes feelings, teaching emphasizes thinking..

In present day family life, child psychologists advise parents to teach their children, rather than preach to them. Popular phrases like, "When I was your age, I had chores to do and didn't have time to hang out at the Mall, sit for hours at a computer, or do all that texting." Such language constituted preaching, not teaching.

Apparently, a clear distinction between preaching and teaching cannot be made without taking into consideration variables such as context, culture, era, translation, psychology, religion, morality, and ethics. Even then, the distinction remains somewhat blurred.

Perhaps a final question should be, "Does any real or imagined difference between preaching and teaching have an applied meaning? If so, what is that meaning?

CHALLENGING THE AGE BANDIT

nthropologists suggest that we are the only creatures that have a sense of mortality. It is not how long you live, but how you live long. Although satisfaction for most people usually focuses on family, career, and maintaining good health, the length of one's life continues to get the most attention.

People are living longer today than they did a century ago. Career-changes at age forty or fifty are not uncommon. Adult education has encouraged senior citizens to go back to school. The increase in leisure time and early retirement has become big business. If longevity continues to increase at its present rate, it will create problems in areas of healthcare, housing, and social welfare.

If pharmacological research were to create an immortality pill, it is interesting to speculate how many people would be willing to take it? Most people would not. Their main reason would be that everyone they know and love would be dead. The few who would relish living forever are not dissuaded by the thought of leaving behind their loved ones and starting life anew.

A memorable film that addressed immortality was titled, "The Picture of Dorian Gray" written by Oscar Wilde. In it, a young man named Dorian Gray has a painting of himself in his attic that spares him the ravages of aging; He remains young, while the painting undergoes the effects of aging.

Plastic surgery is a popular method of counteracting the effects of aging. Every part of the body can be minimized, maximized, or entirely eliminated. Since most procedures do not constitute a medical necessity, they are not covered by insurance,

In some cultures, aging is viewed with more compassion and respect. The elderly are extended the reverence they deserve because of their wisdom and life experience. Unlike America, they are rarely moved into a nursing home.

How should the value of a life be measured? Should it be based upon the accumulation wealth, property, and influence, or a dedication to the overall welfare of society?

In every generation, there are individuals who want to make a difference. Most people live a traditional life eating, sleeping, working, and raising a family.

Many cultures believe that death is not an end, but a new beginning. In the Judeo-Christian religions, it is called the afterlife. The deceased ascend to a variety of abstract locations; e.g., Heaven, Paradise, Nirvana, Valhalla, Happy Hunting Ground, or the Elysian Fields. One of the more interesting places described in the Germanic religion is called. Valhalla. is reserved for valiant warriors. There, they drink liquor that flows from the utters of a goat, fight each other every day with the slain revived in the evening, and feast on the flesh of a boar slaughtered daily and made whole each evening.

Most people do not view death and dying optimistically. They try to make every day count. In an effort to delay the inevitable, they endeavor to eat sensibly, exercise, and think positively.

Here are some ways to successfully defeat the age bandit. Stay in touch with family members and old friends, seek professional help when needed, have regular medical check-ups, don't become a couch potato, avoid negative-minded individuals, watch comedy shows on television, take a rejuvenating afternoon nap, refrain from dwelling on your symptoms or on how things used to be and, lastly, smile more and frown less.

WE ALL HAVE A STORY

We all have a story inside us waiting to be told. Maya Angelou puts it this way, "There is no agony like bearing an untold story inside of you." History is a series of stories. Your personal history is also a story. While there were stories you inherited, that are no longer relevant, it soon became incumbent upon you to create your own life story.

It is important that you do not underestimate the value of your story, think that others will find it uninteresting or boring. When you belittle or trivialize your story, you become incapable of thinking new thoughts, seeing new opportunities, lighting new lamps.

In a bygone era, oral stories were shared with one person or a small group. Today, storytelling has been democratized. Communication media such as Face book, Twitter, Email, and YouTube have given millions of people a voice, a platform to tell their story.

Philosopher Marshall McLuhan coined the phrase, "Global Village." In his books, he suggested that people around the world could now communicate with one another; share their stories. The story Anne Frank tells of her struggle to survive during WW 11 now has a universal audience.

If you ask someone the right question, it often opens a floodgate of information about what they think, feel, and believe. A good question is, "What was your greatest achievement?" Another is, "What one word best describes your life?" Questions like these open the pages of their untold story. All they needed was a patient and interested listener.

It is a mistake to think that only the stories famous individuals have to tell deserve to be told. Every story, be it one of a lonely or abandoned child, a handicapped shut-in, or an individual struggling with the onset of Alzheimer's, each comes with a heartrending story.

Most people take their untold story to their grave. Despite their efforts, survivors have difficulty putting remembered pieces of the deceased's story together.

In 1939, at the World's Fair in Flushing, Long Island, a Time Capsule was buried containing stories of life in the early 20th century to be opened in 5000 years. The objective was to share current stories with future generations. Without stories, the past is quickly forgotten. Our stories contain lessons on how to improve the quality of life on our tiny planet.

Those who keep a diary or a journal are creating a story. Their intent is not for others to read in the future, but as a catharsis, a means of venting personal fears, apprehensions, and anxieties. Their inner voice desperately wants its story to be heard.

Some of the stories people harbor contain a pathological secret, something they have never revealed – never told another soul. Usually, it is something of which they were embarrassed or ashamed.

The famous Mark Twain stipulated that the contents of his will should not be revealed for a century following his death. In it, he said sacrilegious things like, "I cannot see how a man of any large degree of humorous perception can ever be religious -- unless he purposely shut the eyes of his mind and keep them shut by force." or, "A man is accepted into a church for what he believes and turned out for what he knows."

The stories of ordinary people are more optimistic. They usually consist of memories of which they are proud and that others would find uplifting.

Two things give our life meaning. The stories we tell and the ones we leave behind. In the end, everyone's story is open to a different interpretation. One man's success is another man's failure, one man's trash is another man's treasure. Every story is unique.

POWER OF NEGATIVE THINKING

C onventional wisdom has always led us to believe that positive thinking is constructive and negative thinking, destructive. Most people assume that optimists outperform pessimists because they have a high level of confidence and high expectations. The objective of negative thinking is not about giving up or being pessimistic, but to focus on what gets in the way of constructive thought. If sensibly applied, negative thinking can convert anxiety into action.

Psychologists remind us that uncertainty is what motivates negative thinking. By imagining a worst-case scenario, pessimists are motivated to prepare more and try harder. Optimists subscribe to the certainty principle implying that they know all that needs to be known in a given situation and require less preparation. Without an ability to eliminate the positive and accentuate the negative, to ignore the actual and explore the possible, we will remain helpless captives of the past.

Overly ambitious and unrealistic positive thinkers can be a danger to both themselves and others. Realism isn't positive or negative. It requires a careful consideration of all constructive and practical options.

Negative thinkers are more in touch with reality than positive thinkers. The future is uncertain and more things go wrong than go right. Positive thinkers tend to ignore Murphy's Law; i.e., "Anything that can go wrong, will go wrong." They convince themselves that all will go well and that success is inevitable. Philosophers call them Pollyannas – people who think good things will always happen, that there is something good in everything. Negative thinkers, conversely, confront future surprises, rather than pretend that they do not exist.

Negative and positive thinking are both capable of producing disastrous results. Ideally, a balance should be struck between optimism and pessimism.

It is difficult to refute the arguments presented by Dr. Norman Vincent Peale in his world renowned book, The Power of Positive Thinking. Critics called the book a cotton candy theology that proposes an unrealistic response to life distracting people from attending to real social issues. Given this negative criticism, how does one explain it being translated into fifteen languages and selling seven million copies?

How we think is the basis upon which civilization has been founded, the manner in which it has evolved, and how it impacts upon life in the 21st century. Our survival depends upon whether we are negative or positive thinkers.

Historically, every event was contingent upon whether a leader was a positive or negative thinker, an optimist or pessimist, a realist or a dreamer.

Today, every issue confronting America will depend upon how members of congress and how our president thinks. Our destiny may be determined by their attitudes, values, and beliefs. Albert Einstein put it his way: "We cannot solve our problems with the same thinking we used when we created them."

MARRYING OUT OF YOUR SPECIES

In the Old and New Testament, marriage is between a man and a woman. Even among the prehistoric cavemen, a connubial relationship was between men and women.

Through the ages, this interpersonal arrangement remained the norm. Humans consistently married another human. While factors such as culture, race, and religion mediated this relationship, heterosexuality remained the norm. Only recently has same sex marriage become a heated social and legal issue. Currently, in several states, it has become legal.

When the Puritans landed at Plymouth Rock, they brought with them values that were narrow-minded and strictly enforced. It was unacceptable for people to marry someone of a different religion, race, or gender.

Since changes in these social and cultural norms were inevitable, we have now come to a horrendous stumbling block, marrying out of your species. There are a great many people who value their pets more than they value people. There are pet cemetery throughout Florida where their beloved pets can be afforded the same respect and dignity in death as humans.

Today, specially trained assistance animals provide therapeutic benefits to humans with physical and mental illnesses. They become dearly loved and treasured companions. Wild West stories of cowboys and their horses tell of similar relationships that would put many human relationships to shame.

What are the ingredients of a good marriage? Love, respect, loyalty, tenderness, compassion, and emotional support are key elements. Be honest. Which of these qualities could not also be provided by a devoted dog or cat? With the exception of bestiality and an inability to have offspring, interspecies marriage is a viable alternative. Should the inability to have children be a major issue, there are countless human couples who turn to adoption. Why couldn't an interspecies couple do the same?

Opponents of interspecies marriage insist that because animals use a different method of communication than humans, they would not be able to communicate. That is not true. Nonverbal communication is an excellent means of communicating with an animal using touch, body movement, eye contact, gestures, smell, vocalics, and facial expressions. They are all excellent means of communicating.

Current laws make no provisions for an interspecies marriage. You cannot walk into a local marriage bureau with your beloved basset hound or cocker spaniel and request a marriage license. They will gladly issue you an alternative dog license.

Since we presently have the benefit of transsexual surgery, computerized life support, synthetic food, genetic engineering, cryonics, and space travel, why not interspecies marriage? None of these would have been conceivable or available a century ago. Unless we abandon our anthropocentric view of the world, and extend other species equal footing, we may be imposing a serious limitation on our survival as a civilization.

There was a time in America when interracial marriage was not legal. In 1967, the Supreme Court legalized it. There was a time when transsexual couples could not become legally married.. Now, they can. The next hurdle will be allowing transgendered couples to marry.

As a devout iconoclast, I am suggesting that interspecies marriage is on the horizon. So many things that were previously deemed impossible have since come to pass. We have come from candles to atomic power, horse drawn buggies to manned rockets into space. The term impossible should either be removed from our dictionaries or more realistically redefined.

IMAGINARY ILLNESS

_{⸺⸺⸻ ⸨◈⸩ ⸻⸺⸺}

P
eople who imagine they have various symptoms are medically classified as hypochondriacs. Despite all their medical tests being negative, they insist that what they are feeling is real. Many make the rounds of doctors until they find one who agrees that what they feel is real.

While this condition was previously considered to be a mental problem, recent studies now treat it an anxiety disorder. Since its symptoms are not under a person's voluntary control, they can create a great deal of distress and markedly interfere with an individual's normal everyday function.

While the nature of these imaginary symptoms can be extremely varied, common ones include extreme fatigue, headaches, stomach noise, difficulty breathing. or mysterious pains in a body part. If they are convinced that their headaches are due to a brain tumor, and an MRI fails to reveal one, their belief remains unshaken.

Hypochondriacs are not faking. They honestly believe that they are sick and that their symptoms warrant medical attention. The longer their symptoms prevail, the more emotionally deep-seated they become.

What causes these imaginary symptoms to initially occur is not clearly understood. Medical theorists suggest a history of sexual abuse, an inability to express emotions, having a parent with the disorder, or a hereditary predisposition.

There is no magic bullet that will cure hypochondriasis. Most often, sufferers are referred to a psychologist or psychiatrist.

The reason why the condition is so difficult to treat is because hypochondriacs harbors an unshakable belief that their condition is real, not caused by a fanciful imagination. Ultimately, the treatment of this condition is predominantly supportive, rather than curative.

CORPORATE MEDICINE

L ife consists of an endless series of choices, what to eat, where to shop, how to rear our children, etc.. However, when it comes to our health, our ability to choose suddenly becomes seriously compromised.

Profit is the linchpin that fuels commercialized healthcare. An elimination of the profit motive would cause the medical profession to experience a serious collapse. With little warning, corporate medicine has progressively commandeered how patients are treated in clinics, hospitals, and by private physicians.

Currently, physicians are rewarded for prescribing unnecessary medication, ordering expensive diagnostic tests (CT-scan, MRI), seeing a greater number of patients in a given period of time, have needless surgeries, and making inappropriate referrals to specials. If they do not fulfill these corporate incentives, they stand to have their income compromised or, in some cases, their position.

What physicians object to the most is having their expert medical opinion with regard to how a patient should be treated overruled by non-medical personnel. In particular, healthcare insurance administrators.

Charitable non-profit institutions that offer free medical care to the poor, or otherwise economically disadvantaged, are succumbing to the number of "for-profit" healthcare facilities currently monopolizing the healing arts. As a result, it has become increasing more difficult for non-profitable patients to be admitted and treated in emergency rooms. If they can't pay, they are turned away.

On balance, corporate medicine does offer patients some benefits. Supported by governmental grants to further research, significant breakthroughs are made in the treatment of Parkinson and Alzheimer disease, muscular dystrophy, and spinal chord injuries.

There are two phrases that corporate medicine should embrace. The first is, *salus aegroti suprema lex* – meaning, the welfare of the sick is the supreme law. The other is, *primum nil nocere* -- do no harm. If these two principles were actualized by corporate medicine, disease will have met its most formidable adversary.

ARE WE INHERENTLY SELFISH?

I n 1976, Richard Dawkins published a book titled, <u>The Selfish Gene</u>. It addressed the role that selfishness plays in our life. He suggested that we are driven to survive by our genes. We follow our own self-interest in order to survive and procreate. Our genes enable us to adapt more easily to a competitive world at the expense of the others. Success usually requires a certain degree of selfishness.

For centuries, philosophers and social scientists have tried to resolve the paradox between altruism and selfishness. Can an altruistic individual commit a selfish act and, conversely, a selfish individual commit an altruistic act? People are not one type or the other. Many factors determine how they will behave in a particular situation.

Historically, selfishness has been condemned and, in some cases, punishable. A closer look at selfishness reveals its positive aspects.. Every human being has the trait of wanting things that others have. Envy fuels selfishness. Even death reveals an element of selfishness. When someone dies, tears are shed because they are no longer around to provide the survivor with love, friendship, care, and financial support.

This raises an interesting question. Do completely selfless acts exist? Why would a complete stranger dive into a river to save a child? Would the satisfaction from committing such an altruistic act satisfy the ego of a selfish person? Being selfish does not mean that a selfish person cannot commit a selfless act.

The human race is selfish, hardwired to survive. Altruism is learned. It is not an inherent trait. Altruistic behavior can give meaning to a person's life. They do not volunteer out of kindness and compassion. They do it because it fills an emotional void.

In the business world, studies have shown that individuals who act in their own self-interest are more likely to gain dominance and leadership recognition than those who exhibit altruism. Selfish people tend to take better care of themselves instead of giving too much energy away serving the needs of others. Putting yourself first is not a negative quality; it's your job to take care of yourself and get what you need."

WHAT YOU DON'T KNOW ABOUT PAIN

Your perception of pain influences how you experience it. For example, there are individuals who sustain serious injuries and report having very little pain. Conversely, there are those who sustain only minor scrapes or bruises and act as though their life had been threatened. This has been observed in battle where a soldier misinterprets the extent of his wounds. Even though he has a compound fracture of his leg and is bleeding profusely, he tells the attending medic that he feels little or no pain.

The brain is capable of relegating pain to a recessive state; a filtering process. During a football game, a player might sustain a serious sprain or fracture and not be aware of it until the game was over. It is not unusual for people to get bruises and not know from where or when they came. The brain prioritizes incoming pain sensations and raises the more important ones to a conscious level and stores less important ones in memory.

Because hypochondriacs focus an exaggerated amount attention on real or imaginary pain, they perceive it to be worse than it actually is. To a lesser extent, ordinary people who dwell on their pain amplifies their perception of it.

Anxiety, fear, and a loss of control all contribute to how pain is perceived and a reduced dependence upon pain-killing drugs. Having more control of how their pain is managed seems to make their pain more tolerable.

Since pain thresholds vary, it is incumbent upon healthcare professionals to respect how much pain a patient claims to be feeling, rather than what the physician or nurse considers an appropriate response. They should make a special effort to create a nonthreatening environment by keeping needles and other equipment needed for an injection out of sight. Instead of saying, "This shot will cause some initial pain," they should say, "There will be some mild discomfort." Whatever can be done to distract a patient's attention away from a painful procedure will help reduce their anxiety and apprehension.

What most people do not realize is that pain is a learned experience. Viewers watch television programs that depict how criminals react to the pain they experience during an aggressive police interrogation. Or, how patients manage their pain during a debilitating illness. From sources like these, suggestible individuals are conditioned to react to pain in a particular way.

Television commercials also warn viewers to be on the lookout for a variety of painful symptoms. They increase the impact of their message by having actor-doctors attest to their seriousness.

Pain is an irrefutable phenomenon. If you say your back hurts or that you have a headache, those pains cannot be disproven. While there are certain tests that physicians claim produce varying degrees of pain, they do not unconditionally prove that you do not have those pains.

To illustrate that our ability a control how we react to pain is real, we have to understand what enables certain people to walk on hot coals, insert long needles into varying parts of their body, or swallow swords. Some say they are magical tricks. Other myth busters have validated that these feats are really a case of mind over matter. During hypnosis, stage performers have repeatedly demonstrated how, people under hypnosis, will register no response to painful stimuli. Certain dentists have clinically demonstrated that they are able to perform various painful procedures without anesthesia, but by having a patient hypnotized and given the post-hypnotic suggestion not to feel the pain.

How we react to a pain is not simply a knee-jerk phenomenon. Scientific studies have recently discovered how the brain manages pain. When you stub your toe, the sensory nerves in your toe send signals up to your brain via your spinal cord. There, connections are made with areas that control memory, biochemical releases, voluntary and involuntary muscular actions, metabolism, imagination, creativity, and a host of subconscious information.

What does all this mean? It means that pain is not some magical or mystical event. There is no pain genie hiding in your mind. You can, to some extent, control your pain.

A FAITHFUL PET IS A TREASURE

D evout pet lovers claim that their dog or cat is more loyal than any person they know. When a man comes home from work, his treasured pet greets him with boundless enthusiasm, never reprimands him for being late,. Children find their pets always ready to play.

A growing body of evidence confirms that pets invest their owners with better mental and physical health. Research also indicates that pet lovers have lower blood pressure, suffer fewer heart attacks, have less feelings of neglect and hopelessness, and recover more quickly from surgery.

A woman, who hadn't spoken a word for several years, shocked visitors from a local canine therapy group by turning to her caregiver and saying, "Very nice dog."

Terminal ill patients are less likely to suffer from depression if they have animals around them. Animals seem to promote a significant level of comfort and support,

One hundred and thirty-eight pet owners with diabetes reported that their dog began whining and barking when their blood sugar became dangerously low. At a Paris hospital, they found that a certain breed of dog, a Belgian Malinois shepherd, could be trained to detect prostate cancer by smelling the urine of a man with that disease.

Dolphins have also played a therapeutic role with disabled children. They are easy to train, are very social, and love to play, Every time a child was allowed to pet, hug, kiss, stroke, or swim with a dolphin, it lengthened their attention span, ability to focus, level of self confidence, motor skills, and cognitive thinking.

Why do we love our pets? There seems to be a deep-rooted reason why humans surround themselves with dogs and cats and other animals. New research suggests that we are hardwired to our pets. The genetic mechanism that makes us do that probably dates back millions of years when vertebrates were first evolving.

Regardless of the kind of pet, whether it be a dog, cat, horse, or dolphin, pet therapy has become an invaluable member of the medical community. Their loyalty, obedience, sensitivity, and willingness to serve those who love them makes them a distinguished member of society. The famous author, Anatole France, put it best when he wrote, "Until one has loved an animal, a part of one's soul remains unawakened."

BAD NEWS EXCEEDS GOOD NEWS

O n any given night, television presents seventeen cases of bad news to one of good news. Why viewers find floods, murders, forest fires, volcanic eruptions, theft, financial catastrophes, earthquakes, sexual perversion, and terrorism so fascinating has baffled psychologists for years..

Experts suggest that our brains evolved in a hunter-gatherer environment where an immediate response to an attack by a saber-tooth tiger was necessary for them to survive. Perhaps this tendency has carried over into our present day response to any form of bad news. We care about the threat of bad things more than we do about the prospect of good things; we are more fearful than happy. The unusual piques our curiosity more than the usual. Headlines that say, "Alligator bites off child's leg or avalanche swallows up twelve mountain climbers" immediately gets our undivided attention.

The most plausible explanation of why we are mesmerized by bad news is because it is not happening to us. We subconsciously count our blessing. The media counts on us feeling this way.

The uplifting and heartwarming television shows of the fifties, sixties and seventies like. Happy days, Little House on the Parairie, The Partridge Family, Father Knows Best, the Cosby Show, the Donna Reed Show, and the Andy Griffith Show. have all given way to the likes of Silence of the Lambs, Criminal Minds, CSI, The Waking Dead. and Breaking Bad. .

On one of the 5 major networks there is at least one show every night that graphically shows people getting murdered or being the victims of crime. Terror spills out of almost every channel.

A great many people have become so fed up with seeing all that blood and gore, they have turned to reading a good book, listening to soothing music, or doing the crossword puzzle.

Because there is so much bad news in the media, people have become desensitized, so numb that they are no longer shocked by foul language or seeing someone's head chopped off.

In Gone With the Wind, audiences gasped when Clark Gable said, "Frankly, my dear, I don't give a damn." The word damn in those days was forbidden by the Film Production Code. Today, the filthiest language is common in film, stage, and television. Commercials blithely speak of erectile dysfunction, vaginal salves, hemorrhoids, and Viagra to invigorate sexual intercourse.

It seems that morality in America has sustained a lethal blow. Bad news is common currency, while good news is an endangered species.

THE HISTORY OF KISSING

I s kissing an inborn or invented human trait? Scientists suggest that it is inherent because chimpanzees give one another pecks on the lips, snails caress each other with their antennae, birds touch their beaks. Only humans and our evolutionary cousins the Bonobos (the pygmy chimpanzee) engage in full-fledged tongue-to-tongue lip hockey.

There are all kinds of kisses. In the mafia, there is the kiss of death (bacio della morte), Catholics give one another a kiss of peace, Jews kiss the Torah, gamblers kiss the dice before they throw them in craps, Judas kissed Jesus, and enraged individuals sometimes demand that a kiss be planted on their buttocks.

Not all cultures engage in kissing. In Darwin's book, The Expression of the Emotions in Man and Animals, he observed that kissing was replaced by rubbing noses in various parts of the world. Early explorers noted that, in the Arctic, the Inuit people rubbed noses.

Many cultures didn't know about kissing until they encountered the Europeans. The Lapps of Northern Finland would bathe nude together, but did not kiss. The Europeans brought kissing to China, but the Chinese regarded it as a disgusting and vulgar practice.

Some historians have suggested that it is only within the last 800 years, with the advent of modern dentistry and the triumph over halitosis, that the lips were treated as erogenous zones of sexual excitation. Sigmund Freud associated kissing as a return to the sucking of a mother's breast. Women today, color their lips in much the same way certain animals present themselves when they are in heat.

Kissing probably began as a means of creatures smelling one another. It has also been suggested that humans have a distinctive scent that is recognized by an intimate partner. One imaginative writer suggested that the honeymoon is over when the kiss that was once an invitation becomes an obligation. Another creative writer proclaimed that at twenty, a kiss is an experiment, at forty, a sentiment, and after that, a compliment.

The way people kiss varies with the times. In Gone With the Wind, Clark Gable kissed Scarlet O'Hara by simply pressing his lips against hers for a prescribed length of time. Today, kisses are much more explosive involving elaborate lingual and lip gyrations.

Kisses can be spontaneous or intentional. In the fairytale, Sleeping Beauty, the intentional kiss that awakens her is delivered by a handsome prince. A spontaneous kiss is one that a woman might experience from a perfect stranger at a New Year's Eve party when the clock strikes twelve.

Putting aside all the theories about how and why people began kissing one another, the bottom line is that it feels good, depicts affection, denotes a relationship, and seals a deal.

Three quotes do justice to a kiss. "A kiss is a lovely trick designed by nature to stop speech when words become superfluous."(Ingrid Bergman) "If we spoke with our ears, and listened through our mouth, then a kiss might be the most romantic sound in the world." (Jarod Kintz,). "The first kiss can be as terrifying as the last." (Daina Chaviano).

MISTAKES ARE LESSONS
TO BE LEARNED

I t is difficult to imagine what the world would be like if no one ever made a mistake. Whatever the task, correcting a mistake always brings a sense of satisfaction. Picture an athlete trying to execute a particular gymnastic move and, after several unsuccessful attempts, finally succeeds. Only someone with a loser mentality regards a mistake to be irreversible.

George Bernard Shaw insisted that the man who never made a mistake, never make anything. Sensible individuals make mistakes, learn from them, and move on. Those who are excessively preoccupied with a mistake get so paralyzed by guilt, they end up doing nothing.

Failed attempts often create a self-fulfilling prophecy; i.e., what you were afraid would happen, actually happens. A more optimistic approach produces just the opposite outcome.

Most mistakes can be explained through the use of logic and common sense Although most people know better, they continue to make the same mistakes over and over again. This may be due to how they feel, rather than how they think. Most mistakes are driven by emotions, not by intelligence.

Mistakes are either intentional or accidental? Was the mistake due to something beyond the individual's control?

Whatever the reason, the outcome is what counts.

Our evolution is riddled with and crippled by a long line of mistakes. It was once a mistake to think that the world was flat, that blood did not circulate, that the Earth was the center of the universe, and that germs did not cause disease. Today, we look back on what people used to regard as fact as nonsense. Imagine someone in the year 1885 saying that he had landed on the moon. Such an individual would probably have been considered insane. Today, astronaut, John Glenn, could say that he walked on the moon and we would simply smile and be proud to meet him.

Mistakes are discouraging. Ironically, we learn more from our mistakes than from our successes. Adding insult to injury, we are usually remembered for what we did wrong than from what we did right. One thing done wrong cancels out ten things done right.

Should children be encouraged to view a mistake as something positive, something from which they can learn, something that will improve their chances of future successes? Or, does making a mistake create an indelible stain on a child's self-image?

Will future generations have to suffer the consequence of mistakes we make today? Will global warming and environmental pollution come back to haunt us? Every discipline makes mistakes. They are the ingredients that make technological and industrial growth possible. The excuses we make for our mistakes is extremely important. Those who make mistakes, and refuse to correct them, are predisposed to making them again. Old ways die hard. Because change involves some degree of risk, most people perceive it to be a threat.

Mistakes are wake-up calls that prompt us to focus on something that has gone wrong. Psychologists encourage us to treat mistakes as signposts that put us on the right path.

These words by Dr, Steve Maraboli capture the essence of making mistakes. "We all make mistakes, have struggles, and even regret things in our past. But you are not your mistakes, you are not your struggles, and you are here NOW with the power to shape your day and your future."

DIFFERENCE BETWEEN MALE
AND FEMALE DOCTORS

I t has been estimated that by 2017, there will be more female physicians than male. Researchers account for this giant leap in womankind to their spending more time with their patients. Overwhelmingly, women prefer obstetricians and gynecologists of their own sex. In addition to spending more time with patients, they tend to be more encouraging and reassuring. Because of this tendency, male medical students are beginning to avoid these specialties.

When females entered medical school in the 70s, they were encouraged to deemphasize their femininity by wearing slacks, rather than skirts. However, since the feminist movement, sex-specific dress is no longer an issue.

Many female patients still feel uncomfortable presenting themselves in various stages of undress before a strange male who happens to be wearing a white coat and has a stethoscope hanging from his neck.

In a Chicago hospital some years ago, a female patient registered a complaint against her male physician for unnecessarily exposing her. He entered the room, nonchalantly drew back the bed sheet covering her, lifted up her gown, and proceeded with his examination. During the inquiry that followed, the physician's defense was, "The disease was under her nightgown."

Because of their parental approach, male physicians tend to interrupt their patients more frequently when they are speaking. As a result, a growing number of patients prefer the open-ended and interactive relationship that can be had with a female physician. Because they are less reluctant to ask questions, they appreciate the opportunity to play a more active role in their treatment..

Research also indicates that female physicians are better listeners. An MRI study showed that both sides of the female brain is involved in listening, whereas with males, only one side.

Years ago, there was a popular conundrum that circulated in the field of medicine. A father and son go fishing, and on the way home they're in an auto accident. The father is killed instantly. The boy is rushed to the hospital, where the surgeon takes one look at him and screams, "Oh, my God, it's my son!" What is the relationship between the surgeon and the child? Obviously, the surgeon is the child's mother. The moral of this anecdote is that, back then, people only considered doctors to be males, not females.

In making a distinction between male and female physicians, competence is seldom an issue. There are good and bad doctors in each category. Difference usually involves attitudes, values, and beliefs related to the practice of medicine.

While there is still a residual stigma associated with male doctors physically examining women in obstetrics and gynecology, it is no longer a prohibitive issue in medical practice. Nevertheless, a growing number of women are currently displaying a preference for practitioners of their own sex.

In the early days of television, there were no female doctors. Shows like Dr. Kildare, Ben Casey, Marcus Welby, Mash, and Doogie Howser, were all male-dominated.

In 2001, the tide shifted with a show called, Crossing Jordan and a series of other female dominated doctors; e.g., Three Rivers, The Mob Doctor, Bones, Grey's Anatomy, and Private Practice.

Given this cross-section of male and female physicians, the next step is robotic doctors where gender is irrelevant. Will differences between robots then become controversial?

Credit
Andrew Johnson

MATTER OVER MIND

Age is a case of mind over matter.
If you don't mind, it doesn't matter.

Satchel Paige

H ere, I prefer to reverse the "Mind over matter" axiom. Unlike the heart, liver, or spleen, there is no anatomical organ called the mind. It is an abstract term used to describe what the brain does. Phrases like losing one's mind or being out of your mind have meaning only in terms of the behavior they induce.

Current research by neuroscientists have succeeded in discovering specific neuro-synaptic circuitry responsible for memory in the hippocampus of the brain. By manipulating a biochemical substance called neurotransmitters, they have been able to block certain memories and trigger others.

Somehow, our brain is able to filter the synaptic patterns sparked by incoming stimuli and conscious thoughts into our short and long term memory. Researchers have also succeeded in isolating individual neurons associated with a specific image; e.g., Marilyn Monroe or Halle Berry. Remembering something from the past can bring to life the same brain cells that were initially experienced.

Apparently, our brain can trigger a particular memory independently, or it can be triggered by a conscious thought; an interplay of mind and matter. It makes us wonder whether we cry because we are sad or are sad because we cry.

Did you ever try to <u>not</u> think of an elephant? It is impossible because, in order to do it, you must first think of an elephant. Clearly, not all of our thoughts are consciously initiated. You can be lying in bed and, suddenly, the name of a friend you haven't seen for many years pops into your mind. Scientists have been unable to figure out what causes these images to spontaneously occur. In religion, figures like Joan of Arc is said to have experienced an epiphany. One theorist speculated these to be her words: "I must be at the King's side... there will be no help (for the kingdom) if not from me. Although I would rather have remained spinning [wool] at my mother's side... yet must I go and must I do this thing, for my Lord wills that I do so." Historically, many others have had a similar experience. Is it all due to matter over mind or mind over matter? Do we control our neurons or do our neuron control us? If all human thought and behavior can be attributed to how our neurons behave, it could be said that, "We are our neurons.

In 1936, Alan Turing, a mathematician and code-breaker, conceived of a theoretical machine that could carry out any mathematical operation. In effect, it became the forerunner of artificial Intelligence. To test his hypothesis, he challenged an observer to tell the difference between the thinking of a human being and that of a machine. It became known as the "Turing Test."

A later version of the Turing Test experiment involved having a human compete with a computer in a game of chess. Its purpose was to see if the machine could fool its human competitor into believing that he was competing with another human instead of a computer. Scientists concluded that thinking in the brain isn't really that much different from thinking in a machine; i.e., matter over mind.

DEFINITION, DEFINITION, DEFINITION

O ur perception and conception of everything can be traced too how a word or phrase is defined. The terms right or wrong, good or bad, fact or fiction have all shaped and continue to shape the way we live life.

Most religious wars hinge on how scriptural texts are defined. What usually lessens their credibility is the absence of an explicit context. Terrorists are notoriously guilty of taking things out-of-context.

Racism is an example of definitional hypocrisy. The word "black" often denotes negativity such as the black market, blacklist, and blackmail. White denotes less negativity in terms of cowboys wearing a white hat, white lies, and white collar crime. During WW II, Adolph Hitler designated Joseph Goebbels as his chief of propaganda. He defined the word "Jew" in the most racially egregiously way.

In the early West, native Indians were defined as savages. To make matters worse, the Supreme Court in 1923 decided that people of Indian descent were not white men, and thus not eligible to citizenship.

In academia, definitions also play an active role. Terms like tenure, scholarship, literacy, and assessment are defined differently. Professors have been fired because their publications were not deemed scholarly. Schools have been denied funding because the Department of Education defined "grade assessments" differently.

Pollsters have significantly affected the outcome of an election and of administrative appointments on the basis of how terms such as competence, experience, and character are defined.

In the liberal arts, careers have been made or destroyed on the basis of how their peers defined the quality of their work.

Any effort to refute the importance of definitions is doomed to failure. Socrates wrote, ""The beginning of wisdom is the definition of terms." As of November 2014, the full Bible has been translated into 531 languages. What further proof is needed to validate the critical roll played by definitions

IS SWEARING BECOMING LEGITIMATE?

S wearing and cursing is not new. What is new is its incidence. It can now be openly heard in shopping malls, restaurants, business establishments, and by a staggering number of teenagers. According to a language watchdog group called, Parents Television Council, profanity on television increased more than 500 percent from 1989-1999. Since then, that percent has markedly increased. What is most disconcerting is that it has invaded prime-time family programming.

To illustrate how far we've come with regard to what constitutes foul or obscene language, audiences gasped when Clark Gable, said, "Frankly, my dear, I don't give a damn" in 1939,

The words damn and hell were never mentioned on TV until <u>All in the Family</u> debuted in 1971. Today, they are regular fixtures on network television and deemed completely harmless.

In 1972, Comedian Georg Carlin's legendary routine, "Seven dirty words" was not allowed on television. Carlin countered by saying, "There are 400,000 words in the English language and there are seven of them that you can't say on television. The ratio is. 399,993 to seven." He begged the question, "Why is society so offended by the arrangement of three consonants and a vowel?"

For a long time, children were chastised for using certain language in the home. Parents threatened to wash their mouths out with soap. This practice no longer exists because many previously dubbed dirty words are no longer considered dirty.

Since the Federal Communication Commission's power to regulate broadcasting standards has been seriously challenged in the courts, television profanity is up 69 % and climbing. Family and cartoon programming are also succumbing to obscene language.

In Ashley Montague's book, The Mother Tongue, he attempts to make us more aware of how language should be approach and how certain dirty words came into existence.

In time, profane words and phrases have become demystified and the public is no longer offended by them. To make them less offensive, a list of euphemisms have been invented such as darn, durn, goshdang, jumping Jehoshaphat, and many others. Nevertheless, habitual swearers continue to insist that euphemisms fail to deliver the emotional satisfaction they get from using taboo expletives;

Language expert, Jessie Sheidlower, explains that there are 109 different targets of offensive language such as religion, sex, race, ethnicity, politics, and body parts.

Although a great many people are still offended by the arbitrary use of offensive language there is scholarly research that points out its positive aspects. For example, swearing relieves painful pent-up emotions and serves as a substitute for physical violence. It prevents people from feeling like victims by increasing their self-confidence.

Humorous swearing among friends can be an enjoyable pastime and create a sense of community.

Swearing improves circulation, raises the level of endorphins, and creates a sense of calm, control, and well-being. Mark Twain had this advice with regard to swearing, "When angry, count to four; when very angry, swear."

There is an interesting phenomenon associated with people who suffer from Tourette's Syndrome. It is called coprolalia. It is characterized by the patient uncontrollably blurting out a series of curse words or phrases completely out of context. Some deaf patients suffering from Tourette's Syndrome have been reported to swear in sign language, where it is called copropraxia.

Although the incidence of swearing has increased significantly, it is doubtful whether we will ever see it completely disappear. What will probably happen in the foreseeable future is that previously offensive words or phrases will either disappear or be replaced by more creative euphemisms.

THINGS THAT DIVIDE US

People have always been drawn to those who look, think, and act the way they do and are repelled by those who do not. Xenophobia is the word that illustrates this form of social discrimination.

Biologically, what lies beneath our skin is essentially the same. Psychologist Abraham Maslow created a paradigm he called, Hierarchy of Needs. At its bottom he lists our most basic needs (food and shelter). At its top, our most challenging need (self-actualization – the ability to fulfill our potential).

What, then, divides us? Traditionally, it has been differences in language, religion, types of government, behavioral norms, history, and our values. It is difficult to think of any war that did not include one of these constructs. Wars feed on differences, not similarities.

Instead of a willingness to peacefully respect and tolerate differences, we have traditionally resorted to violence. Almost every era is identifiable by its wars or confrontations. Future historians will characterize America by citing the wars and military operations in which it was involved.

At the turn of the century, former President Theodore Roosevelt said, "I should welcome almost any war, for I think this country needs one." Fulfilling his prophecy, the US Special

Operations Command in 2013 reported that the U.S. had special military operations forces in 134 countries. Since the United States was founded in 1776, she has been at war during 214 out of her 235 calendar years.

Because so many people have difficulty resolving their differences, conflict resolution, anger management, and critical thinking courses are now being offered in colleges and in the workplace. These courses stress: talk less, listen more, stay focused, try seeing things from the other person's perspective, stay calm and give positive feedback by saying, "I see exactly what you mean." Above all, avoid using "You Messages" which are judgmental or accusatory. Instead, use "I Messages" in which you say what you feel and how you respect the other person's opinion.

In most cases, differences are triggered by emotions, rather than by logic or rational discourse. Frustration is a common side-effect that could make violence the only viable solution.

THE DEMISE OF HUMILITY

B etween 1660 and 1700, Richard Allestree's book, <u>The Whole Duty of Man</u> went through fifty-six editions and 200,000 copies devoting only thirty-six pages to humility. Jonathan Sacks, a leading rabbi in England, called humility the "orphaned virtue of our age." Today, humility continues to be a stepchild of interpersonal communication.

Despite our struggle to arrive at a clear-cut definition of humility, it has been defined as the death of the self, the end of desire. It is the way we relate to others and, in the process, create a sense of oneness. The famous author and journalist, G.K. Chesterton, wrote, "It is always the secure who are humble." Helen Keller, who spent her life being deaf and blind, was far from feeling secure. And yet, her profound intellect, will, and compassion, prompted her to write these sage words: "I long to accomplish great and noble tasks, but it is my chief duty to accomplish humble tasks as though they were great and noble. The world is moved along, not only by the mighty shoves of its heroes, but also by the aggregate of the tiny pushes of each honest worker."

A well-nourished self-image is a valuable asset. Only when it is overblown that it creates hubris, an excessive pride and arrogance.

What quality traits should a humble person possess? In Matthew 5:5 it is written, "Blessed are the meek, for they shall inherit the earth." Does this conception of meekness differ from ours? Should our leaders and elected officials be meek? Should meekness be defined as a mild or quiet temperament, or should it be taken to mean someone who lacks initiative and is rather submissive?

It is doubtful whether there is a prenatal humble gene. There may, however, be a character or personality trait that facilitates humility. Growing up, children tend to emulate their parents. If one or both parents are strong-willed, extroverted, and outgoing, there is a high probability that their children will behave similarly. When parents are kind and mild-mannered, their children will probably model their gentle nature. In both cases, there will always be children who exhibit behavior opposite to that of their parents.

Can humility be taught? While many books describe people who were humble, few deal with ways to become humble. The best way of learning humility is to seek out those who possess it and imitate them.

It is wrong to regard a humble individual as someone who, when faced with adversity, routinely turns the other cheek. Humility is not a synonym for weakness.. The Dali Lalma of Tibet, and the Reverend Desmond Tutu, Archbishop Emeritus of Cape Town, Africa, are both men of great inner strength and are taken to be humble. Their behavior denotes their humility.

Humble individuals are usually non-threatening because they tend to be open-minded, resilient, tolerant, and not adversarial. Mahatma Gandhi was humble, but he was also extremely adversarial, steadfast in his views, and of very strong character; certainly not meek.

Are ego and humility compatible traits? Few people would think Mother Theresa had a big ego. We think of her as the epitome of humility. Yet, she had a huge ego - a powerful self-image allowing her to stand before the world convinced of her truth, convinced of her worth, and convinced of her importance. It takes a powerful ego to do that and yet, she was humble.

Although humility, in various interpretations, is seen as a laudable virtue, that was not the case in ancient Greece where it meant something like "crushed" or "debased" and was associated with failure and shame.

True humility is not thinking less of yourself, it is thinking of yourself less. Brian D. McLaren confessed his impassioned humility with these words, "I'm sure I am wrong about many things, although

I'm not sure exactly which things I'm wrong about. I'm even sure I'm wrong about what I think I'm right about in at least some cases."

Unless the clarion call of humility is answered, traits such as pride, arrogance, narcissism, and intolerance will have won.

EXCREMENTAL COMMUNICATION

E xcrement comes in all shapes and sizes. The clinical study of feces is called scatology. Aside from feces being an indispensable use as a fertilizer, it plays a prominent role in medicine helping physicians diagnose certain illnesses. Linguistically, there are four terms associate with feces: Coprophilia and copromania both signify an obsessive interest in feces. Coprophobia is an abnormal fear of feces. Coprolalia is an uncontrollable and excessive use of scatological language (example is Tourette's Syndrome). Coprology is an obsession with feces and defecation especially as expressed in art and literature. Overall, the focus is on feces or, more colorfully put, shit!

Stubbing your toe, bumping your head, or having your fingers caught in a closing door receive little or no emotional relief by blurting out words such as darn, golly, drat it, gracious me, or shucks. The preferred expletive is usually "Oh, Shit!" The same exclamation might be heard from a man unable to extricate his car stuck in a large snow bank. In both instances, the operative word is shit; definitely a multi-purpose linguistic tool.

It is questionable whether the word shit is class-specific; i.e., used more liberally by members of a particular class of people. Casual observation does suggest that it is more prevalent among the less educated where vocabularies are shorter.

Language is a tool that should be used according to a given situation. Labeling certain words dirty and others clean detracts from the efficacy of language. What was once considered improper might now be considered proper.

Etymologists have traced the word shit back to Old Norse (Skita). The North German word "schiete" also means shit. The acronym S-H-I-T was once suggested to stand for "Ship High in Transit." All words have a history and, in order to fully appreciate their meaning, one must become aware of their origin and cross-cultural interpretation.

For some curious reason, the word shit has not enjoyed the benefit of a good reputation. Despite efforts by the film industry to restrict the use of certain foul or vulgar language, and a wide variety of other licentious scenes, its control didn't last too long. Insidiously, the industry became progressively more permissive and less restrictive.

According to Wikipedia, the word "fuck" is used 506 times in the film, The Wolf of Wall Street.' In Spike Lee's 1999 film, Summer of Sam, fuck was used 435 times. On radio, the FCC doesn't pursue any broadcasters unless a complaint is made. Someone could say "fuck" on the air, and if nobody files a complaint with the FCC, nothing comes of it.

What determines the offensiveness of a word? Is it's sound or the physical image it generates in the mind? Take the word GUANO. Technically, it means bat shit – an excellent fertilizer. However, those who market the product prefer to call it Guano, rather than writing the words "Bat Shit" on its container..

How far behind is our language in terms of today's morality? It would be interesting to see how mainstream universities define proper language. For instance, would a college in the bible belt (The South and Mid- West) define it differently than one in the North East?

In Ashley Montague's book, The Mother Tongue, he explores the role of swearing in a scholarly manner. He attempts to make readers aware of how one should approach language by acquiring a better understanding of how certain dirty words came into existence. He insists that knowing this defuses future resistance and contempt for certain words that are simply ink marks on a page or a series of vocal utterances. Semanticists repeatedly alert us to the fact that words have no meaning; that all meaning is in us and it is only in the mind that linguistic tolerance can be found.

AUTOEROTICISM

I f it feels good, and not physically or mentally harmful, do it! Self-stimulation for sexual pleasure has existed since we appeared on this planet. Although references to masturbation has not been found in early cave paintings or other prehistoric artifacts, it has been observed among Bonobo chimpanzees, which share 98.4 percent of our DNA.

Despite the bad press it has traditionally received, masturbation continues to play a prominent role in human experience The Judeo-Christian attitude toward masturbation stems from a myth called, "The sin of Onan." According to Jewish law in biblical times, a brother was expected to procreate with his brother's widow. Onan, refusing to comply, spilled his seed on the ground, hence the term Onanism, which was taken to mean masturbation.

For this spurious reason, masturbation, homosexuality, and oral-anal sex has been routinely denounced as wrong, evil, and against God. During the 17th and 18th centuries, masturbation received its first social stigma. It was said to cause insanity, visual and hearing problems, epilepsy, and mental retardation. So prevalent was the notion that between 1856 and 1932, the U.S. Patent Office awarded 33 patents to inventors of anti-masturbation devices. Some of the names under which they were marketed included Simple Bondage, Leather-Jacket Corset, Spike-lined Ring, Stephenson Spermatic Truss, Bowen Device, the Cage, Dr. Moodie's Apparatus for Boys. Penis-Cooling and Sexual Armor. All were designed to prevent males from masturbating.

Upon entering the 20th century, the masturbation issue underwent a turn for the better. The Kinsey Report in 1948, served to demystify the practice of autoeroticism. Not only was masturbation no longer considered harmful, but normal and an excellent means of reducing sexual anxiety and frustration. Because Surgeon General Jocelyn Elder in 1994 suggested that masturbation is part of human sexuality and should be taught," President Clinton fired her.

The ancient world of the Egyptians celebrated masturbation and believed that the sun god, Atum, created the first Adam and Eve equivalents, Shu and Tefnut; "With the hand of God, Atum masturbated and brought forth the first pair of souls." During that same period, Sumerians believed that the Mesopotamian god, Enki, masturbated and his ejaculation filled the Tigris River with water.

Although masturbation has been subjected to an historical juggernaut, it has managed to come through with flying colors. This is especially significant at a time when the Aids epidemic has made millions of adults wary of indiscriminant sex. As a result, masturbation has become an inexpensive, safe, and convenient alternative.

According to Nobel Prize winner, Max Planck, "A new scientific truth is seldom won by convincing its opponents, but because a new generation grows up that is familiar with it." Today, despite continued religious opposition, masturbation, homosexuality, and oral-anal sex appears to have come out of the closet. Cable television has absolutely no qualms about openly airing programs dealing with these topics. Almost every type of sexual behavior has found a receptive audience in a significant part of the general population. The film industry, in particular, has gotten on the band wagon. Yesterday's taboos have been expunged from today's literature and the performing arts. Its stigma has lost its sting. Again: "If it feels good, and is not physically or mentally harmful, do it!" But not in excess.

THE IMMORALITY OF WAR

There is only one way to
abolish war forever and
that is to have WW III.

N othing in human experience surpasses the insult that war
imposes upon humanity. Was Darwin right when he wrote
about survival of the fittest?

The concept of war has long challenged the imagination of
philosophers. Repeatedly, they ponder these questions, "Why do
people resolve their differences by going to war?" What is there about
war that cancels out other more peaceful alternatives? Is the human
brain defective? Was something in the evolutionary process a mistake?

On a recent television panel discussion consisting of journalists
and authors who covered the Viet Nam war, a statement by one of
the panelists struck a nerve. He said that in every war, each side is
ignorant of its enemy's cultural history, norms, needs, and social
profile. Writers have suggested that, in order for soldiers to kill an
enemy, it was necessary to dehumanize them; i.e., create an image that
was abhorrent, reprehensible, and viscerally offensive. They must be
perceived as vermin, scum, dregs of humanity. Hitler characterized
Jews in this manner.

Although there are historical pockets of peace on Earth, they
are few in number. War seems to be more compatible with human
propensities than peace. People invent differences and it is over these
differences they are willing to kill one another.

It is unlikely that there will ever be world peace. Not unless there is a worldwide inoculation of people to make them behave in a certain controlled way. The film "Stepford Wives" (1975) illustrated this phenomenon. Men in the film created a biological strain of women that would be completely subservient to their every wish.

Revolutionaries who advocated change have traditionally been exiled, executed, excommunicated, tortured, or ignored. On only rare occasions have their altruistic endeavors been realized and seldom in their own lifetime.

Regardless of the label assigned to a revolution, the worst thing is that the right people are seldom killed. Finley Peter Dunne hit the nail on the head when he wrote, "The trouble with war is that all the preliminaries are arranged by matchmakers. All they have left are the fighters to do the murdering."

The etiology of man's penchant for war has caused some researchers to attribute it to high levels of testosterone, a substance facilitating such anti-social behaviors as toughness, status, dominance, and violence --- qualities essential to a soldier's basic training. Imagine a college graduate in accounting, philosophy, or business administration being drafted into the armed forces in WW II. How is he transform into a killing machine – something contrary to his nature. How is this transformation accomplished? In 1940, the Selective Service and Training Act enabled the armed forces to induct, in just one month, sixteen million young men. Did all these young men possess the inherent qualities necessary to turn them into killers?

The nature of war has changed dramatically in the past century, Traditionally, wars were fought by men. Women now constitute a significant number in every branch of the military. Can women be conditioned to kill as readily as men? The feminist movement in the United States has changed all that arguing that women and men should be treated as equals.

In next war, gender will be irrelevant because it will be fought by pressing a computer key, not on a battlefield. To end WW II, President Truman had to make a monumental decision; i.e., whether or not to drop the atomic bomb on Hiroshima and Nagasaki. No more landing on foreign beaches like Iwo Jima, Guadalcanal, or Normandy. All someone in an aircraft named Enola Gay had to do was to push a button. This one act served to end WW II..

No discussion of war should end without asking whether there is anything redeeming about war. This difficult question involves issues dealing with morality, ethics, and especially, religion. No one reading the New Testament can come away from it without an awareness of the role war has played in its evolution. This goes for the Old Testament as well. Rarely does one read about peaceful conflict resolution, where leaders sat down and calmly discussed their differences. In the Book of Joshua, God told Joshua before he entered the Promised Land (Canaan) to slaughter all the infants and to kill off every living thing. On numerous other occasions in the bible, figures who were, ostensibly, able to communicate with God, were instructed to commit some rather violent acts in his name. These events are certainly not consistent with a search for peace on Earth, goodwill toward men.

Regardless of how certain violence-prone individuals rationalize war, the reality is that they exist and will continue to exist for the indeterminate future. What we should do is focus on what these despotic individuals are disseminating. Leaders are powerless without followers. Wars are fought by those whom they indoctrinate and not by the leaders themselves.

Wars are avoidable, but not without a concerted effort by peace-loving individuals to educate themselves, become more aware and sensitive to the rhetoric of those advocating war. If it weren't for the millions of Americans who actively protested the Viet Nam war, it would have lasted a great deal longer.

Marshall McLuhan said we are now living in a global village. We can no longer think of ourselves in insular terms. Globalization means connectedness, directly or indirectly. What happens in one part of the world has the capacity to effect other parts. Violence has a powerful voice that resonates easily. Television and computers act as linchpins facilitating a worldwide awareness. A scant hundred years ago, people in Chicago, New York, or Los Angeles, didn't have a clue as to what was going on in China, San Salvador, Iraq, or South Africa. Today, the entire world plays out in our living rooms on the evening news.

The axiom, "I didn't know that" is no longer an excuse for professed ignorance. It is incumbent upon all those who abhor war to become informed, know what is going on in the world and, if at all possible, make their opinions known. War is a choice and, in the final analysis, choice is all we have – something for which men have given their lives – freedom of choice. What you don't use, you lose.

Anyone seriously interested in reviewing the literature on war will encounter a morass of contradictions. Wars have been committed for an endless collection of assorted lies, misrepresentations, and myths.

All world leaders who ever declared war were convinced that they were right and God was on their side. Whatever their rationalization, it was always taken to be right by their protagonists and wrong by their antagonists.

Perhaps our species would be better served by learning how to effectively cope with war, rather than complain about it. While this may sound like a defeatist attitude, it could represent the only viable option. Why? Because if all is fair in love and war and fair play is the name of the game, humanity is inescapably trapped in a no-win situation.

PERSEVERENCE

‑‑‑‑‑‑‑‑‑‑‑‑‑‑‑‑◄《◉》►‑‑‑‑‑‑‑‑‑‑‑‑‑‑‑‑

D on't be discouraged. It is often the last key in the bunch that opens the lock. If you are confronted by a problem, have tried a number of possible solutions and not been successful, perseverance will ultimately save the day. History and common sense bears out this simple truth. Your stubbornness, your unwillingness to give up, will be your reward.

Those who have been successful in every walk of life, under the most trying circumstances, are avid supporters of perseverance. They all encourage that people find the intestinal courage to hang on, stay the course, ride out the adversity.

Perseverance is not a hereditary ability. It requires will power, dedication, determination, and a generous helping of motivation. Perseverance is the missing element in the mind-set of unsuccessful individuals with talent.

If Louis Pasteur, Alexander Graham Bell, Marconi, Michelangelo, and Leonardo Da Vinci, lacked perseverance, the world would have been deprived of their invaluable contributions.

A most compelling example of perseverance is the <u>Harry Potter book</u> by J.K. Rowling. Twelve publishers rejected the manuscript! A year later she was given the green light by Barry Cunningham from Bloomsbury who agreed to publish the book, but insisted she get a day job because there was no money in children's books. What if Rowling had stopped at the first rejection, the fifth, or the tenth?

Perseverance is not easy. People invent a variety of excuses to justify quitting, Thomas Edison said, "Many of life's failures are people who did not realize how close they were to success when they gave up." Perseverance rarely comes in short periods of time. More often, a lifetime commitment.

In healthcare, those stricken by a debilitating illness are challenged to keep faith in their physician, reach deep inside themselves and discover an unknown source of perseverance they didn't know existed.

Most people underestimate their talent, intelligence, and inherent congenital gifts. Helen Keller is a familiar example. At 19 months of age, she developed either scarlet fever or meningitis that left her deaf, blind, and mute. With the help of Anne Sullivan, she persevered enough to earn a college degree, become a well known author, political activist, and sought-after lecturer. The famous actor, Christopher Reeve, who played Superman in film, became a quadriplegic after being thrown from a horse during an equestrian competition. Confined to a wheelchair for the remainder of his life, his perseverance enabled him to lobby on behalf of people with spinal cord injuries, plus a number of other laudable social services.

Albert Einstein had this to say about perseverance. "Nothing in the world can take the place of persistence. Talent will not; nothing is more common than unsuccessful men with talent. Genius will not; unrewarded genius is almost a proverb. Education will not; the world is full of educated derelicts. Persistence and determination alone are omnipotent. The slogan Press On! has solved and always will solve the problems of the human race." Perseverance makes all things possible.

ARE YOU XENOPHOBIC?

D
o you prefer the company of people who look, act, and think the way you do or those who are different? If your social preference favors similarity, you might be xenophobic. Because we are now living in a multicultural society, people who are racially, culturally, linguistically, and religiously different, incline to ghettoize. When Chinese, Italian, German, Swedish, Spanish, British, African, and Irish immigrants landed on our shores, they established small replicas of the countries from which they emigrated. Despite their differences, they slowly became acculturated and perceived themselves as Americans. Some, however, preferred to retain their ancestral identity.

The term xenophobia (derived from the Greek) refers to attitudes, prejudices and behavior that rejects, excludes, and often vilifies outsiders or foreigners to the community. Based upon this definition, being called a xenophobic is an insult.

During its first year, newborn infants perceive no difference between themselves and other infants. If placed in front of a mirror, they typically smile, coo, and delight in having their movements bounce back at them. Shortly thereafter, their perception of differences become more pronounced.

Xenophobia is a learned, rather than an inherent trait. In childhood, many parents warn their children to avoid playing with children who are different. Impressionable youngsters soon came to regard this discrimination as acceptable and normal behavior.

In a 2000 TV series titled the Twilight Zone a segment featured a group of people with only one eye. One day, a woman appeared among them with two eyes. Immediately, their xenophobia prompted them to remove one of her eyes to make her look normal.

Logic or critical thinking cannot justify xenophobia. During WW II, Adolph Hitler convinced the German people to hate Jews. He succeeded in converting an entire population into cruel and vicious xenophobes who, in concentration camps, inflicted heinous crimes against innocent men, women, and children.

Throughout our entire history, xenophobic emotions have been responsible for the loss of well over 100 million lives. The world Thomas More conceptualized in his famous book, Utopia, is an illusion, A world devoid of xenophobia is unrealistic.

The most reprehensible example of xenophobia was the way early colonists treated the indigenous American Indian. In what constituted genocide, the colonists eliminated approximately 95% of their population and deported survivors to reservations.

Africans brought to America as forced laborers suffered a similar fate.. They were perceived to be uncivilized and forced to worship Christianity and observe European traditions.

In the late 1840s,. Chinese workers arrived in large numbers to help build the railroads that would form the backbone of the emerging U.S. economy. To illustrate their perceived inferiority, they were portrayed as cooks and servants in film and in the early days of television.

Since the early settlers of America were initially immigrants., it is ironic that they should feel threatened by present day immigrants.

In 1984, Reverend Jesse Jackson founded the National Rainbow Coalition, a social justice organization devoted to political empowerment, education and changing public policy toward people who were racially and culturally different.

Like other phobias, xenophobia is treatable. A first step is to make sufferers more aware of how their behavior is hurting and harming others. The next step is exposing them to examples of how xenophobia impacts on the tranquility of a civilized society. The Golden Rule, "Do unto others as you would have them do unto you" is the most powerful antidote to xenophobia.

THE VALUE OF A GUESS

For centuries, guessing has had a bad reputation. From the earliest grades, up to and through college, guessing has been discourage. Students are trained to stay with known and well established information. In history classes, they were cautioned to accept the contents of history books *carte blanche*, without question; Columbus discovered America, Washington threw a silver dollar across the Potomac, or that Marie Antoinette actually said, "Let them eat cake."

Today, the art of guessing has been resurrected and afforded a much deserved respect in every discipline. Even though Albert Einstein was pretty smart,. he didn't arrive at his famous equation E-MC2 by complex mathematical reasoning. He made it up. Without any proof, evidence, or scientific reasoning, he woke up one morning and said "It's got to be so." He simply guessed it.

The famous physicist, Richard Feynman, encouraged scientists to do more guessing. He followed by saying that guessing alone is meaningless. It must be subjected to rigorous experimentation. If it disagreed with experimental findings. the guess was wrong.

Judging the reliability of sources found on the Internet is crucial because there is no regulating body that monitors its credibility. Someone who ventures a guess as to what Melville originally had in mind when he wrote <u>Moby Dick</u> can turn the story into an animal rights issue with impunity. According to historian Will Durant, "History is mostly guessing, The rest is prejudice."

When a distinguished or reputable individual ventures a guess, it is often taken to be true, rather than mere speculation of conjecture. If President Obama comments on global warming, the public is unable to discern whether he is basing his opinion on hard environmental evidence or his connotation of its significance.

Differentiating a guess from a fact is not easy. Clever politicians can often disguise a guess by immersing it in ambiguous language. The best defense against unsubstantiated guessing is to question everything. Having blind faith in what you see, hear and read makes you a sitting duck by those seeking to manipulate gullible individuals; i.e., *Caveat lector* (let the reader beware).

CURED OR HEALED

B eing cured simply means the removal of symptoms. Being healed is to make whole the mind, body, and spirit. Put another way, you can cure without healing and heal without curing. In medical school, students tend to focus more on curing than healing. Sydney Burwell, former Dean of Harvard Medical School, said, "Half of what you are taught in medical school will be wrong in 10 years." The trouble is that your teachers don't know which half.

While fractures, sinus infections, and gastric ulcers are easily cured, migraine headaches, hypertension, cancer, diabetes, fibromyalgia and emphysema are not.

Sophisticated advances in surgery are based on the premise that by removing its effects like a lump in the breast, a leg with an osteogenic sarcoma, or a brain tumor, the patient is cured. These procedures are done without knowing what caused them. Etiology is a term that refers to causes. Most patients don't realize that the practice of medicine is based largely upon theory, supposition, and guessing. Visiting a dermatologist with a rash that won't heal often involves trying various salves and ointments until one works. This form of treatment is often done without knowing what caused the rash. If the dermatologist is asked for an explanation, the answer might consist of consuming a particular food, contact with an irritating agent, or simply stress. Invariably, the cause and effect riddle is challenged.

In a famous textbook on pathology by William Boyd, he writes in the Foreword, "After performing hundreds of post-mortem procedures,

I am constantly amazed at how many people can live symptom-free lives with so many undisclosed disorders."

Despite the mystery behind health and disease, we should continue to have faith in our current healthcare providers. Their intentions are sincere and well-meaning. The history of medicine is filled with nooks and crannies of discovery. Overall, we are now blessed with the ability to transplant a heart, correct cataracts, re-attach lost limbs, and create mechanical prostheses enabling wounded veterans to live a meaningful life.

Salus aegroti suprema lex means, "The welfare of the patient is the supreme law."

FEAR OF BEING ALONE

F eeling oceanic, a term coined by Sigmund Freud, is to feel that life has lost all its meaning. Other terms characterizing the fear of being alone include feeling abandoned, alienated, disconnected, disenfranchised, isolated, or depressed. It is an emotion with which most people have difficulty coping. Unlike hypertension, heart disease, diabetes, or anemia that are successfully treated with medication, there is no "magic bullet" for feeling alone. Only antidepressant drugs such as prosaic or valium can dull the feeling.

The cartoon character, Pogo, says, "I have met the enemy and it is me." Another related axiom asserts, "A problem well-stated, is half-solved." Both of these familiar sayings strongly suggest that anyone who feels lost has the reason for their depression lodged in their brain. Ironically, if misperception can create an oceanic feeling, it can reflexively uncreate it. Fear is not an enemy, but a compass pointing in the right direction, an opportunity to recover from emotional distress.

What causes people to feel lost? Is it the loss of a job, an unpleasant divorce, menopause, a debilitating disease, getting old, an unfulfilled career, or a financial crisis? People cope with these trials differently. Some see the proverbial glass of water half-full, others see it as half-empty, some see trees, but not the forest.

Aside from relying on pills to lessen their despair, there are several available remedies: joining a support group, exercising regularly, good nutrition, volunteering, meditating, yoga, professional counseling, social outreaching, and getting enough sleep. Each of these will help ease the impact of feeling lost.

By itself, feeling lost is not a sign of mental illness. It is only when such an overpowering feeling makes an individual incapable of self-care that professional help is appropriate.

Feeling lost comes with pitfalls. It is a psychological trick the mind plays to insulate an individual from having to deal with an unpleasant issue. While such a mental maneuver may produce short-term relief, it should not rule out a need for professional help.

Many people get stuck in the muck and mire of unfulfilled dreams. Their lives are overtaken by an invisible automatic pilot. Getting unstuck requires disengaging the pilot's tenacious grip. The deepest hunger in life is for a secret that is revealed when a person is ready, willing, and able to appreciate its revelation.

Henry Thoreau reminded us that it is not until we are lost that we begin to understand ourselves. Feeling lost is a paradox – an opportunity to do something that requires all the courage an individual can muster. Only, then, can a positive change occur. To the question of why you feel lost, you are the answer, the only solution.

Historically, extremely talented people get so completely immersed in their work that contact with the outside world becomes impossible. They become lost in their own private world of creativity. At times, we all go through a transient fear of being alone We must learn from the experience and move on.

DANGER OF SELF-DIAGNOSIS

The cardinal rule in medicine is to never base a diagnosis on just one symptom. For example, there are individuals who test positive for AIDS and show no symptoms of the disease. There are patients with cancer who have no symptoms and appear the be in good health. In these cases, their immune system is strong enough to maintain homeostasis; a high level of resistance.

Googling creates an irresistible temptation to self-diagnose. Gullible viewers often identify with one symptom mentioned by an actor-doctor and immediately head for an advertised over the counter remedy. Without the medical background of a physician, the tendency can be extremely dangerous. It may delay the administration of proper medical care.

Self examination of the female breast can be misleading.. The female breast normally consists of an abundance of fatty tissue which, when explored by a medically untrained hand, can frighten a woman into thinking she has breast cancer.

A thirty-five year old man felt a bump at the bottom of his rib cage, something he had never noticed before. Thinking it might be a tumor, he made an appointment to see his primary physician. On the examination table, the doctor asked him to point to the bump that worried him. He was greatly relieved when the doctor said that the bump was the normal bony end of his sternum. Because his self-diagnosis was based on an ignorance of normal human anatomy, he was unnecessarily upset.

While doctors encourage their patients to become aware of any bodily changes, they are discouraged from jumping to conclusions. While this advice is medically sound, its effect is compromised by the misleading onslaught of television commercials designed to make viewers think they have every known disease ranging from leukemia. to leprosy.

The number of misdiagnoses made each year is staggering. A recent commentary on a Texas Veteran Administration. estimated that with more than a billion primary care visits made annually, a half-million are missed diagnoses. If such a poor batting average occurs in such a large medical facility, image how often the average physician makes a wrong diagnosis.

What does all this mean? It means that self-diagnosis is at the bottom of the barrel. Most people have a distorted perception of both their physical appearance and how their body works. When asked to point to their liver, a majority of people are mistaken. This simple truth make self-diagnosis a dangerous practice for the average person.

Before doing your next self-diagnosis, here are some things to bear in mind. Online health sites are not regulated. The information is compiled by non-medical paid writers. Users tend to focus on symptoms, rather than risks. Punching in a single symptom of abdominal pain could come up with 140 possible causes including colon cancer. Many products recommended may come from unknown manufacturers and fail to contain ingredients written on the label.

Self-diagnosis undermines the role of your doctor. Discuss what you have gleaned from the Internet and if you are still unsure of how to proceed, get a second opinion.

DIRECTIONAL DYSLEXIA

A staggering number of people in this country consistently get lost. Despite having driven to a favorite restaurant many times, they forget whether to turn right or left at a certain junction, on which side of the restaurant the entrance is located, or where they parked the car.

This problem has also been referred to as geographic dyslexia, spatial dyslexia, directional disability, dysgeographica, and dysorienta. Sufferers break into a cold sweat when someone says, "You know how to get home – just reverse direction." They know how to get from A to B, but not from B to A.

Unless they write something down, step by step, they repeatedly get lost, make the same mistake, and become frustrated when they are told to think logically or use common sense. Its like telling a colorblind person that if they focus, pay attention, and concentrate, they should be able to tell the difference between shades of yellow and blue.

Directional dyslexia has nothing to do with an individual's intelligence. In fact, it frequently afflicts people who are very smart. It is conceivable for a brilliant rocket scientist or a Nobel prize winner in astrophysics to suffer from dysgeographica. While they are uniquely proficient in their given discipline, they become hopelessly lost when they have to follow simple directions. They push when a door says pull, enter when a sign says exit, or go north when a sign says south.

Spatial dyslexia in not limited to driving errors. Husbands afflicted with this condition frustrate their wives. They consistently have difficulty finding things around the house. They expect to find something where it was previously located. Any minor change leaves them frustrated and bewildered.

Psychologists have speculated that this problem may be related to a deficit in short term memory or being switched from left to right handedness as a child. Thus far, the puzzle remains unsolved. One researcher suggested that it might be due to late speech development.

Some of the coping measures directional dyslexics use involve keeping a stack of index cards detailing directions to the house of a friends, MapQuest in large print, and memorizing landmarks by associating them with well known images.

Finally, the directionally handicapped frequently rationalize their disability by blaming others for their confusion. For example, if they get lost on the way to a special event, stopping to ask for directions can result in accusing the person giving them directions of being unfamiliar with the area.

The famous Oliver Wendell Homes was not directionally impaired when he wrote, "I find the great thing in this world is not so much where we stand, as in what direction we are moving: To reach the port of heaven, we must sail sometimes with the wind and sometimes against it - but we must sail, and not drift, nor lie at anchor. Even though we might be sailing in the wrong direction, wrong direction is better than no direction."

HEALING POWER OF HUMOR

n ancient proverb reads, "Laughter is to the soul what soap is to the body." Soap cleans the body, laughter cleans the soul." According to the Mayo Clinic, laughter is no joke. It relieves stress, reduces muscle tension, strengthens the immune system and relieves pain. Fifteen minutes of laughter a day can improve an individual's overall health and their attitude toward life. Studies show that heavy laughter increases the level of endorphins in the blood that act as natural painkiller.

In the last decade, hospitals have become convinced that humor does play an important role in healthcare. To implement this belief, certain hospitals have "humor carts" wheeled into a patient's room where they could watch and listen to their favorite comedians. In St. Joseph's Hospital in Houston, Texas, a "living room" was created for their cancer patients where they could enjoy comic films starring the Marx Bros, Ritz Bros, and the Three Stooges. Humor rooms are now available in certain hospitals.

A 1998 film titled Patch Adams, starring Robin Williams, illustrated how a comical approach to the practice of medicine exerts a positive influence on healing. The film received worldwide acclaim.

New York City's Big Apple Circus has used humor to console sick children since 1986 when they started sending teams of clowns into hospital rooms with rubber chicken soup and other fun surprises. Doctors noticed that patients exposed to humor perceived less pain as compared with patients who didn't receive humorous stimuli.

While we are often unable to explain *why* certain situations make us laugh, we certainly feel good when they do. The emotional buoyancy and stress relief brought on by laughter improves our quality of life.

Here are some thoughts that can increase your faith in the healing power of humor: A good laugh is sunshine in the house. Laughter is always available. If you look, there is an element of humor in everything. No antibiotic can compete with a good belly laugh. Suppressed humor is a crime. Laughter serves as an open connection between mind and body. Smiles erase wrinkles; frowns create them. The best medical prescription is: "Take two belly laughs and call me in the morning."

PROPHYLAXIS

Today's healthcare stresses the diagnosis and treatment of disease more than its prevention. Although some physicians stress the importance of prevention, their number is steadily decreasing.

Corporate medicine, along with the pharmaceutical industry, appear more concerned with profit than prevention. Telling people to eat sensibly, get enough rest, and exercise doesn't fill the coffers of organized medicine.

It wasn't that long ago when advocates of healthy living were called "health nuts." Today, that stigma no longer exists. Perhaps the greatest contribution to the health of Americans has been the explosion of Health Clubs or Fitness Centers. Jack La Lane opened the first health club in Oakland, California in 1936, He pioneered ways and means of getting healthier. From 1951 until 1985, his nationally syndicated exercise show on television preached good nutrition and physical fitness. Critics said the show would last less than six weeks; it lasted thirty-four years. Preventative medicine is finally drawing people away from pharmaceutical pill-peddlers. The plethora of drug and disease related commercials on television has made viewers therapeutically paranoid.

Medicine is in a constant state of flux. Ironically, there has been more progress in the surgical sector than in curing a common cold. Aspirin appears to have had the longest dependable lifespan. Many diseases are cyclic; they run their course and mysteriously disappear. Bubonic plague and cholera have been traced to poor sanitation.

Healthcare professionals are guardians of our health and, as such, must always be open to change. The tendency to remain shackled to old and established modes of therapy impedes progress.

One of the most heated prophylactic controversies deals with compulsory inoculation or vaccination. Refutation on both sides have merit. Before parents have their children inoculated, they are required to sign a release or consent form absolving the physician and the drug company from liability. There have been cases where a vaccinated child became autistic. It became a medicolegal issue that still has not been resolved.

Anyone opting to have a prophylactic procedures should get answers to these questions: Does it involve risk? What is its statistical track record? What are the potential side-effects? Is the physician or technician administering the procedure highly experienced?

Prophylaxis has always been and will continue to be an integral part of medical practice. Healing is an art, not a science. Hence, submitting to any kind of treatment is a leap of faith. Oliver Wendell Holmes wrote, "I firmly believe that if the whole *materia medica, as now used,* could be sunk to the bottom of the sea, it would be better for mankind-and all the worse for the fishes."

HOW SUFFERING STRENGTHENS US

S uffering is usually perceived to be an unfortunate human experience. Few people are familiar with its positive attributes. Everything in life is polarized; happiness and sadness, wealth and poverty, moral and immoral, health and disease, and a host of other familiar opposites. We cannot know one with having experienced the other. What would a world be like without suffering? Recent psychological studies tell us that suffering challenges our ability to survive traumatic and often life threatening experiences. A riveting example is Viktor Frankl's ability to survive the unimaginable suffering he experienced in four Nazi concentration camps in WW II. In his award winning book, Man's Search for Meaning, he vividly describes how he was able to psychologically survive the inhuman torture to which he was exposed. Frankl suggests, "There is nothing in the world, I venture to say, that would so effectively help one to survive even the worst conditions as the knowledge that there is a meaning in one's life."

The biblical Abraham, Job, and Peter were all tested to determine their ability to survive various kinds of religion-based trials. In each instance, their suffering made them stronger.

Our entire history is speckled with examples of courageous individuals whose suffering provided their lives with meaning. After being thrown from a horse in 1995, George Reeves (Superman in film), became a quadriplegic. Rather than dwelling on his misfortune, he went on to provide other paraplegics with the courage to lead future productive lives.

Clearly, suffering can be turned from a negative into a positive. When asked to what they attribute their ability to survive, a significant number tell of acquiring a new inner strength they never knew they had. Many spoke of fulfilling a deeply felt need to help others.

The tragic health problems that ruined the life of Friedrich Nietzsche, the famous German philosopher, taught him that when people successfully emerge from episodes of illness and despair, it is as though they are born again and have a renewed faith in the joy of living. The Prophet. Kahlil Gibran, put it this way. "The deeper that sorrow carves into your being, the more joy you can contain."

"There are far too many silent sufferers. Not because they don't yearn to reach out, but because they've tried and found no one who cares." (Richelle E. Goodrich) To suffer alone is to suffer twice.

ARE VERY INTELLIGENT PEOPLE HAPPIER?

----⊶⊙⊷----

"Happiness in intelligent people is
the rarest thing I know."

Ernest Hemmingway

A recent study of 6870 participants reported that people with a high IQ are happier. This finding is meaningless unless the word "happier" is defined. The dictionary defines it as, "Feeling or showing pleasure or contentment."

Do the very smart people you know seem to be happier? When you chat with them, do they appear to be more optimistic, smile more, and take an interest in personal and public affairs?

Highly intelligent people are generally more aware, think more logically, and are better decision-makers. Having these attributes should make them happier. This assumption, however, is wrong. Not infrequently, the media reports a number of such individuals committing suicide.

In a paper delivered by Martin Voracek. a researcher at the University of Vienna Medical School, he suggested that smarter people are more likely to commit suicide. He further discovered that in countries where there was a higher percentage of people with a low I.Q, there were fewer suicides.

Also to be considered is the relationship between intelligence and emotions. Are exceptionally intelligent people less emotional? Does the fact that their emotions and intellect speak a different language affect their psychological disposition?

Does the expression, "You are too smart for your own good." makes sense.? Does the tendency to over analyze everything produce greater emotional stress?

While many very intelligent people live balanced and manageable lives, a surprising number do not. As the study by Martin Voracek suggested, they seem more prone to suicide and depression.

There are a number of disadvantages to being too smart. Some of the disadvantages include intimidating people, becoming easily bored, resent having your beliefs or reasoning challenged, have difficulty making friends, tend to be lonely, and are too self- critical.

J.D. Salinger put it best when he wrote, "I don't know what good it is to know so much and be smart as whips and all if it doesn't make you happy."

DYING WITH DIGNITY

A majority of people feel uncomfortable talking about death and dying. Psychologists tell us that the more familiar you are with something, the less likely you are to be frightened of it. To allay their fear, a free and charitable organization called Die-a-log has been established. It makes a series of public meetings available in which members are invited to share their thoughts and their real life stories that involve death and dying.

Once we appeared on this planet, we have been preoccupied with what happens after we die. Christians speak of heaven or hell. Every culture and religion has created a myth representing the afterlife, a myth with which they are comfortable.

According to philosopher Corliss Lamont, "The wise man looks at death with dignity, honesty, and calm recognizing that the tragedy it brings is inherent in the great gift of life."

In Portland, Oregon, there is an organization called, Death with Dignity National Center. The Center was formed out of a profound commitment to the idea that personal end-of-life decisions should be made solely between a patient, their family, and a physician. The right to die with dignity law maintains that how and when an individual chooses to die is a strictly personal matter.

Aid in dying, also referred to as death with dignity, is currently legal in Washington, Oregon, Montana, New Mexico and Vermont. All other states have laws that prohibit assisted suicide. Is the Declaration of Independence that guarantees us life, liberty, and the pursuit of happiness meaningless? According to Thomas Jefferson, "The care of human life and happiness, and not their destruction, is the first and only object of good government."

For the first time in history, a concerted effort is being made to allow us to die with dignity. In the nineties, Dr, Jack Kevorkian, also known as Dr. Death, assisted in the suicides of more than 130 terminally ill people. He challenged social taboos about disease and dying and, because of his stubborn and often intemperate advocacy of assisted suicide, he helped spur the growth of hospice care in the United States. He made many doctors more sympathetic to those in severe pain and more willing to prescribe medication to relieve it.

An article appeared in the Guardian titled, How Doctors Choose to Die. Because they see all the pain and suffering their terminally ill patients go through, they leave explicit instructions that they should not be resuscitated. They prefer spending their remaining time with loved ones and doing things they would not ordinarily do --- take a trip around the world.

MISUNDERSTANDING EACH OTHER

D espite having over a million words in our language, we continue to misunderstand one another. A huge obstacle is reification; i.e., talking about things that do not physically exist as if they did. For example, we cannot materially touch an ideology. Misinterpreting it has created a breakdown in communication that often pits people against people, nation against nation.

As mentioned earlier, there is no meaning in words, only in people. How words prompt them to behave is all that matters. Action do speak louder than words.

Another barrier to effective communication derives from a conflict between how people think and how they feel. Feelings seem to override thoughts. This occurs when someone looks good, but feels sad or feels sad, but looks happy. This clash between thoughts and feelings can cause a breakdown in communication.

Multiculturalism in America has caused a steady growth in people whose native tongue is not English. As a result, a new obfuscation illiteracy has surfaced. The same word often means something else in another language. For example, Salsa in Korean means diarrhea, peach in Turkish means bastard, fart in Danish means speed or pace, gift in German means poison, kiss in Swedish means pee, preservation in French means condom. This is what causes non-English speakers considerable confusion in ordinary conversation.

Misunderstanding is further compounded by idioms. In America, we have a host of expressions that baffle foreigners. Idioms such as take a hike, off the wall, break my chops, push the envelope, drop me a line, no way, or taking something for granted all serve to confuse them. The problem works in reverse when Italians confront Americans with the idiom, "Che schiavone!" which means "What a big dirt bag or lowlife!" Or, in Spanish, "No tiene dos dedos de frente" which means, "He's not the sharpest tool in the shed."

All the world's problems seem to result from our inability to misunderstand each another. If that is the case, we must proactively address linguistic illiteracy more aggressively.

WHAT MAKES US CIVILIZED?

I s it our language, architecture, technology, religion, or an awareness of our mortality? What, exactly, has enabled us to survive these past few thousand years? This is a question with which philosophers have continually struggled.

There is no simple answer. Each theoretical answer is met with another question. Two of the most popular attempts are the Holy Bible and Darwin's Origin of Species. Although both make an impressive effort, they fail to capture the essence of our existence.

While ethnologists and anthropologists have succeeded in tracking our biological and sociological evolution, potholes remain unfilled.

Our imagination continues to be our only viable window of opportunity. In 1865, Lewis Caroll gave us Alice in Wonderland, In it, Alice encounters a series of puzzles that seem to have no clear solutions, riddles and challenges of life that frustrate expectations and resists interpretation.

Perhaps what makes us civilized is not something out there, but something within us – our brain. Civilization, as we know it, could not exist without a pre-frontal cortex. It orchestrates the core of our cognitive existence.

Sigmund Freud characterized civilization when he wrote, "The first human being who hurled an insult instead of a stone was the founder of civilization." While such a facetious and overly simplistic explanation makes a point, it fails to address the civilized motif in its broader and more complex sense.

Should the label "civilized" pertain to cultures that practiced human sacrifice, torture, and infanticide? Has a line in the sand been drawn that distinguishes between human and inhumane behavior? Are wars to be taken as examples of civilized behavior?

Does what we think or how we behave constitute our being civilized? Does what we think comport with our behavior? Conversely, does how we behave comport with how we think?

It is interesting to contemplate how future historians will describe our civilization. Will they use our Old and New Testament as a yardstick? Unfortunately, there is no Aladdin's Lamp or crystal ball that will answer the question," What makes us civilized?"

WHY TELL THE TRUTH?

T here are times when honesty is not the best policy, when lying and deceit are in an individual's best interest. New research suggests that lying under the right circumstances is ethical, helps to breed trust in difficult situations, and boosts morale.

An example would be to tell your grandmother that you love the sweater she gave you for your birthday. If you were honest, and told her that you didn't like the sweater, it would hurt her feelings.

Four elements constitute a lie: misstatement or untruth, intent to deceive, seriousness of an issue, and a receiver's right to be told the truth. These elements exclude what has been called "social lying" where we flatter people to make them feel good or congratulate a hostess on a boring party. These have been referred to as "little white lies."

In one Gallop Poll, doctors and college professors rated highest on honesty, while lawyers, advertisers, and salespeople scraped the bottom of the barrel. Most respondents voted public officials as the most common liars.

A lie, by any other name, is still a lie. Regardless of whether it is called a whopper, fib, half-truth, or a tall tale, it always boils down to some form of distorted intentional or unintentional meaning.

Because something is not true, it does not automatically qualify as a lie. Consider this statement: "The Earth is flat." While it is clearly not true, it isn't a lie. What would make it a lie depends upon who, why, where, and how it is used.

When people are lied to in a way that helps them cope with a stressful situation, they really appreciate the dishonesty. In healthcare, unless a physician's deception would seriously endanger a patient's life, a compassionate and well-meaning lie could elevate their spirits and speed up their recovery. Physicians who advocate telling a patient the absolute truth seek to insulate themselves from a malpractice suit.

Lies can be verbal, nonverbal, or vocal. A verbal lie is communicated by spoken or written language. A nonverbal lie occurs when a good Samaritan gives a confused motorist help by pointing in the wrong direction. A vocal lie is characterized by people laughing at a joke they really don't think is funny.

Intent is of critical importance in determining the credibility of a lie. Did the liar deliberately tell an untruth? Or, was it unintentional or accidental?

When a witness lies in a courtroom, the judge or jury must weigh the seriousness and context of the lie. Their opinion often affects the degree of punishment meted out.

Pathological liars are people who lie repeatedly. They may or may not be consciously aware that what they are saying is a lie. Technically, the condition is called *pseudologia phantastica* or mythomania. For such individuals, there appears to be a blurring of the boundaries between fact and fiction.

Perfectly normal people lie. Husbands and wives lie to one another, children lie to their parents to avoid punishment, politicians lie to their constituents. Since lying is a worldwide phenomenon, our only defense is to better understand its nature and the role it plays in interpersonal communication.

MY FAVORITE APHORISMS

Philosophers make lousy rulers.
One good question outweigh ten good answers.
Lost items ultimate find us.
Few diseases can compete with a broken heart.
Without analgesics and anesthetics, medicine is doomed.
Our judicial system favors the criminal.
Needs define us.
Politicians are prostitutes.
Relatives are seldom late for the reading of a will.
Never argue with someone who isn't hungry.
War rewards murder.
Human teachers will soon become extinct.
Swearing is an excellent cathartic.
You cannot argue conclusions.
In nursing homes, fond memories keep people from giving up.
Bingo attracts churchgoers more than religion.
Sex is impatient.
It is amazing how many people claim to know what God wants.
Memory is a trickster.
Marriage licenses should be renewed every three years.
There is very little humor in the bible.
A robot running for the presidency is not that far off.
In a nudist colony, genitals are ornamental.
Parenting should be licensed
Prejudice is an equal opportunity employer.

Salaries are rarely commensurate with competence.
To learn about love and marriage, you need different books.
The brevity of women swim suits will soon consist of a raisin.
Teenage vocabularies are pathetic.
Truth is always negotiable.
Knowledge is something you can give away and still keep.
Religion has always been a popular placebo.
Virginity is a hoax perpetuated by men on women.
Future generations will refer to us as savages.
Committees give birth to more committees.
Pacemakers continue to function when you are in a coffin..
Stay out of the kitchen in a fine restaurant.
Lovers never laugh during sex.
One ply toilet paper should be outlawed.
Policemen are legal bullies in blue.

Doing nothing isn't easy.
Quiz shows measure recall, not intelligence.
Nuclear war is inevitable.
Physicians are lazy listeners.
Automatic gratuities on cruise ships is a scam.
On vacation, take twice as much money and half as much clothes.
Mediocrity has replaced excellence.
The internet has become a surrogate parent.
Public tolerance of foul language is doubly offensive.
To a virus, health is a disease.

CAN SLEEP POSITIONS ALTER DREAMS

D o you sleep on your back, side, or stomach? Recent studies deal with the relationship between the position in which you sleep and the content of your dreams. Different positions create physical pressures on various parts of the body that seem to dictate how and what you dream. Those who sleep on their stomach tend to have more intense, vivid, and sexual dreams. Although stomach sleepers are in the minority, their dreams incline to be more erotic.

Left side-sleepers are the most common. Right-side sleepers report more positive dreams and have fewer nightmares. Although back-sleepers are more prone to snoring and apnea, they have more nightmares. They also have greater difficulty remembering the content of their dreams.

Sleep experts discourage sleeping on one's stomach. They say It causes frequent tossing and turning and difficulty finding a comfortable position.

Dreams occur during rapid eye movement (REM-sleep) when the brain is most active. REM sleep usually occurs 3-4 times a night and it is during the final stint of REM sleep that most vivid dreams occur.

Sleep specialist, Chris Idzikowski's research suggests that if you sleep in a bad position, you're likely to be grumpy the next day, if you sleep like a log, you are typically easy going, sociable, and want to run with the A–list crowd. If you sleep on your back with both arms wrapped around the pillow, you are a good friend and always there to be helpful.

Nightmares can be frightening. They usually contain dangerous situations, anxiety, great sadness and physical terror. Waking up from a nightmare makes going back to sleep almost impossible.

For some poorly understood reason, our brain is able to create a separate and distinct world of subconscious experience. Unlike an X-ray or an MRI scan, dreams cannot be observed objectively. Only the subjective recollections of the dreamer are available.

The attempt by current researchers to establish a correlation between sleep positions and dreams is a shot in the dark and should not be taken seriously. Clearly, a great deal of additional research is needed.

COMING TO TERMS WITH
OUR EXTINCTION

T hroughout human history, people have had a compelling desire to know how things will turn out. Prophets, soothsayers, fortune tellers, clairvoyants, astrologers, and sorcerers were all in the business of foretelling the future. It is always interesting to see how seemingly intelligent and educated people still rely on these prognosticators, how they swallow their predictions without question.

A curiosity to know the future is irresistible. This inquisitiveness was especially evident during the Biblical period. To deter the willingness of people to believe soothsayers, Deuteronomy had this to say, "Prophets and dreamers are to be executed if they say or dream the wrong things. 13:1-5; Also, written in Isaiah, "The priest and the prophet have erred through strong drink. You can't even trust a drunken prophet anymore." 28:7.

One of the world's most famous prophets was Michel de Nostradamus, a French apothecary who published collections of prophecies that have since gained worldwide popularity. Most critics of his prophesies (written in quatrains) maintain that they are largely the result of misinterpretations or mistranslations, or so tenuous as to render them useless as evidence of any genuine predictive power. His predictions dealt mainly with disasters such as plagues, earthquakes, wars, floods, invasions, murders, droughts, and battles.

Taken together, the majority of prophecies made throughout the centuries were made by pretenders and revealed as hoaxes. The most popular prophecy has been the end of the world, also known by names such as Armageddon, Apocalypse, or the end of time.

Harold E. Camping, an American Christian radio broadcaster, author, and evangelist, predicted that the world would end in 1994. When that did not happen, he set another date as May 21, 2011 at exactly 6 pm (sunset in Jerusalem). Obviously, that, too, did not happen. Other audacious prophets have wrongly predicted the world to end in 1914, 1915, 1918, 1920, 1925, 1941, 1975, 1994. and Dec. 21, 2012 by the Mayans. What will be the next date? Eventually, one prophecy will be correct, but we will not be around to acknowledge it.

The compulsive desire to know when the world will end will always be with us. When people are asked why they want to know, they usually say it will allow them to make the most of their remaining years. A scientist, priest, and ten year old boy were once asked what they would do if a tidal wave was coming that would destroy the world. The scientist said that he would try to figure out a way to prevent it. The priest prayed for God's intervention. The young boy said, "I would try to find out how to live under water." More optimistic individuals simply wanted the outcome to be a surprise.

Most people live an "As if" life. While their intellect tells them otherwise, they continue to live life "as if" it will go on indefinitely. They refuse to think or talk about a time when their life will end. They find any conversation about mortality depressing. Paradoxically, the thought of humanity becoming extinct does not bode well in the human mind.

There are six questions skeptics usually ask when confronted by a prophecy. Is it credible? Should it be taken literally or figuratively? Is it specific or a generalization? How probable is it? Is the language used consistent with the time in which it was made? What was the prophet's motivation?

No matter how these questions are answered, gullible individuals will still believe them. A closed mind is extremely difficult to penetrate. If the Apocalypse were to come in the form of a global flood, we would need another Noah and his seaworthy craft.

Here is what Paul Watson, a distinguished Canadian environmental activist had to say about our inevitable extinction. "We will lose more species of plants and animals between 2000 and 2065 than we've lost in the last 65 million years. If we don't find answers to these problems, we're going to be victims of this extinction event that we're at fault for."

The difficulty of emotionally preparing for our inevitable disappearance as a species defies rational comprehension. Whatever means each individual chooses will have to serve as their way of coping with the end of times.

WITHOUT PURPOSE, LIFE
HAS NO MEANING

P hilosophers such as Socrates, Plato, Aristotle, and a host of others, have sought the meaning and purpose of life without success. Even the Hebrew Book of Ecclesiastes: 7:-3 offered this opinion: "Man's fate is like that of the animals. All have the same breath Man has no advantage over the animal. Everything is meaningless."

A popular belief regarding life's purpose and meaning is that language determines our thoughts which, in turn, shape the way we conceptualize our world. Since actions usually speak louder than words, perhaps that is where we should be looking for purpose and meaning.

Words and actions often conflict. When people say one thing and do something else, it is called pseudoaffective behavior. The world famous Pentecostal leader, Jimmy Lee Swaggart, is an example. He preached a meaningful and purposeful religious life and practiced something else. His sexual misbehavior in the late 1980s and early 1990s led the Assemblies of God to defrock him.

Any search for meaning and purpose will ultimately be found in an individual's mind. If the purpose of a mountain-climber is to reach the top of Mt. Everest, doing it will only have meaning if he succeeds.

What if you read this headline in tomorrow's morning paper: "Philosophers discover the meaning and purpose of life." First, would you believe it and, if so, would it change the way you are living your life?

Imagine asking the most technologically advanced computer on the planet this question: "Does life have any inherent purpose or meaning?" Now imagine that the answer you get is, "There is now." By simply asking such a question, the computer presupposes an interest in what the words <u>purpose</u> and <u>meaning</u> denote.

Logic cannot compete with faith. Scripture spends a great deal of time attempting to convince readers that the true purpose and meaning in life is dictated by God. Since what is written in the Old and New Testament is based exclusively upon faith, it is irrefutable.

For any discussion on this topic to have value, it must be based upon how the words purpose and meaning are defined. At best, all conclusions ultimately lead back to self-determination, self-image. self-worth, self-esteem, and self-actualization.

NOT ALL DOCTORS ARE PHYSICIANS

T he title of doctor did not always apply to physicians. The first European university, the University of Bologna, was founded as a school of law. The first academic title of doctor applied to scholars of law and did not apply to scholars of other disciplines until the 13th century. In time, the title of "doctor" was extended to include other branches of learning

Fields in which individuals have earned the title of doctor include philosophy, osteopathy, chiropractic, pharmacy, dentistry, and medicine. In England, members of the Royal College of Surgeons drop the title of doctor and prefer to be addressed as "Mister", or "Miss."

Most people, when introduced to someone as a doctor, usually assume that the person is a physician. This is unfortunate because those who have earned a legitimate doctorate in another discipline deserve the same degree of respect.

Another distinction concerns the way those possessing a doctorate view one another. For example, in medicine, despite the fact that they all possess an M.D. degree, specialists usually rank higher than a general practitioner. This distinction also applies to a psychiatrist vs a psychologist.

The field-specific curriculum leading to a doctorate is seldom taken into consideration by the general public. Ears immediately perk up when someone is called doctor. When making a restaurant reservation, deference is usually given to individuals who give their name as Dr. Smith. Even using the title of Professor earns a little more respect.

Tourists visiting Vienna are often confused when they enter a taxicab and are addressed as "Doctor" or "Baron." Dating back to the ancient Hapsburg Empire, titles were taken seriously. Anyone who has attended a university is addressed as "Herr Doctor" or "Frau Doctor." If a person has two degrees, he is addressed as "Herr Doctor Doctor."

The use of titles, in universities, vary. Traditional institutions require their undergraduates to address their professors respectfully; i.e., "Professor Jones or Professor Smith." More progressive colleges now allow their teaching staff to decide how they would like to be addressed. Professors who permit their students to call them by their Christian name (Fred or Larry)" feel that it creates a more open learning environment.

Hospital administrators feel that when patients address their doctors by their first names, it impedes the healing process. While some physicians don't mind being called Joe or Frank, the majority feel that it compromises their credibility.

Each branch of the military has its own particular range of titles. In the army, it ranges from Private to General. In the Navy, from an ordinary seaman to a commodore. In between these extremes are several other titles, each denoting their duties and responsibilities.

In religious circles, there are approximately ninety-five different titles that differentiate its members. Familiar ones are father, rabbi, apostle, bishop, cardinal, chaplain, monk, nun, pastor, and pope. Imagine an elimination of these titles from all religious sects. What would be its effect?

If someone was being introduced to the CEO of a large corporation and, aside from addressing the individual properly, displayed a condescending facial expression, it might prompt the CEO to feel that his authority was being challenged or disrespected. Regardless of the context, social etiquette demands that a legitimate title be given the respect it deserves..

WHAT GOOD IS AN APOLOGY?

An apology is saying the right thing after doing the wrong thing. An unkind word cannot never be retracted. Most of us have said or done things for which we are truly sorry. While expressing our remorse or regret, this declaration should simply increase our awareness of what we have done and remind us not to do it again. It may not, however, heal or remedy the harm it has inflicted upon the person whom we have offended. By acknowledging your shame or regret, you give the person you have wronged the power to forgive you. A perfect apology always requires that it be tailored to the recipient and the situation.

Centuries are filled with apologies having the reputation of being repeated over and over again. But, how should apologists be treated? Should criminals accused and convicted of violent crimes be absolved of their guilt by their simply saying they were sorry? Many a jury member is inclined to vote in favor of a criminal who openly displays contrition and remorse. If the someone committed a pre-meditated crime, under what circumstances should that person be excused?

Jurisprudence takes into consideration such things as intent, the actual act, and its consequences. If someone of sound mind, intentionally, murders a spouse, should the person saying, "I'm sorry" be taken into consideration by a jury? Why? In what way does such an admission make the pain and suffering of the victim any more bearable?

In any apologetic situation, both the apologist and the apologee must be rendered separate, but not equal treatment. The injured party should always be extended greater favor and consideration than the perpetrator. The British author, Gilbert K. Chesterton, had this to say about an apology: "A stiff apology is a second insult. The injured party does not want to be compensated because he has been wronged; he wants to be healed because he has been hurt.

Interpersonal communication often links an apology with forgiveness.. In the Christian confessional, the penitent who expresses genuine regret and remorse for a wrongdoing is usually met with priestly absolution and penance This raises an interesting question: Should such absolution be impervious to the enormity or seriousness of the confession; should it be unconditional? Just how much weight should an apology carry?

Behavioral psychologists place a greater emphasis on what people do than what they say. While the verbal aspect of any interaction should not be ignored or de-valued, actions should always take precedence over words spoken. Humanistic psychologist, Clark Moustakes, leveled this forceful charge: "Accept everything about yourself – I mean everything. You are you and that is the beginning and end -- no apologies, no regrets." While this approach sounds harsh and unfeeling, it squarely addresses the question of responsibility. People who intentionally hurt others, or do things that inflict great harm, should be held accountable. An example must be set so that others clearly understand that such behavior is unacceptable.

We are living at a time in which extraordinary public acts of contrition have become commonplace. One pundit describes the atmosphere that exists in our culture as "apology mania." Public officials, in every walk of life, fill our tabloids with apologies. for various indiscretions. Just how willing should the general public be in excusing their behavior simply because they say they are sorry? While a great many people were willing to excuse their behavior because they ultimately owned up to their actions, the reality is that what they did was wrong.

How should we handle the next apology? Forgive or forget? In most instances, our response will affect, not only our own self-respect and self-worth, but also that of those whose apologies we accept. Ultimately, we will all, at some point, be confronted by the question, "What good is an apology?"

PARENTAL ALIENATION
BY ADULT CHILDREN

T here are parents with adult children who have stopped communicating with them for reasons they are unable to fathom. Such parents must know that they are not alone. There are others, both mothers and fathers, who have similar experiences, and who are in deep agony over the loss of a meaningful relationship with their children.

Although alcoholism, physical or sexual abuse, abandonment, divorce, or emotional instability are among the more common reasons for parental alienation, an unaccountable reason makes the problem especially frustrating..

Not all parental alienation cases end up in court. Many linger for years without a parent knowing why they were estranged by a son or daughter. In some cases, the alienated parent makes several unsuccessful attempts at reconciliation. On advice from friends or relatives, or a professional family counselor, they are told that it is the parent who is obligated to seek reconciliation. The offspring who initiated the disconnect frequently absolve their guilt by blaming the parent.

Ideally, families should remain connected, directly or indirectly, for life. Unfortunately, that is no longer true in America. Self-serving interests have contaminated such a notion. Families are scattered throughout the country.

Estranged parents usually live out an unfulfilled life. Because they have been denied the joy that grandchildren can provide, they envy parents who have such a privilege. To compensate for this void, they often seek out a relationship with other family-related grandchildren. Another approach is to become involved in the parenting role with other children as a Godparent, as an involved uncle or aunt, as a Big Brother or Big Sister. Validating yourself as a parent can go a long way to heal feelings of disappointment.

There are things that can be done to alleviate the sadness associated with alienation. Two excellent methods involve joining a support group and start keeping a journal in which emotional pain is vicariously vented.

Sociologists agree that a majority of children grow into their adult years with a preserved sense of love and respect for their aging parents. There are some, however, who lack this commitment. They claim to have no need for any parental involvement. Conversely, there are those who occasionally experience an epiphany, a revelation, a wake-up call. They realize that life is too short and too precious to continue harboring their inconsiderate feelings; that it is time for them to reach out.

Those who benefit most from this reunion are the grandchildren. Grandparents are a unique breed. Their sole purpose is to generously give their time and energy and expect nothing in return.

There is an interesting Chinese anecdote that illustrates a troublesome father-son relationship. Because they live together, and the elderly father is extremely demanding and a chronic fault-finder, the son decides to get rid of him. He builds a coffin and orders him to get into it. With the coffin in a wheelbarrow, he wheels it to the edge of a steep cliff. As he approaches the cliff's edge, he hears a knocking from inside the coffin. He opens the coffin and the father says, "I know that I have been a tremendous burden, but let me give you some advice. "Save the wood of this coffin because, one day, your son might need it."

Realistically, there are times when reconciliation is impossible. It then behooves the estranged parent to stop trying and concentrate on their own well-being. Some children believe that a reconciliation will open old wounds.

A more hopeful outcome is that, after reflecting upon what life would be without you, the resistant child will become more open to a peaceful elimination of the unhealthy Parent Alienation Syndrome.

VERBAL DIARRHEA

T here are people who have something to say and some that have to say something. What they say is less important than the number and kind of words they use to say it.

Verbal diarrhea refers to people who talk too much and who use unnecessary flowery and obscure language. Other labels such as logorrhea, pedantic, grandiloquence, verbosity, prolixity, sesquipedalia, and garrulous apply to these linguistic exhibitionists.

Here is an amusing example verbal diarrhea:

"The medical community indicates that a programmed downsizing of the total daily caloric intake is maximally efficacious in the field of proactive weight-reduction methodologies."

It could have conveyed the same meaning with the sentence, "Doctors say that the best way to lose weight is to eat less."

George Orwell, author of the famous novels <u>Animal Farm</u> and <u>1984</u> wrote a classic parody of verbal diarrhea. He took a verse from the Book of Ecclesiastes (9:11) and re-wrote it filled with ambiguous gobbledygook.

ECCLESIASTIC VERSION:

I returned and saw under the sun, that the race is not to the swift, nor the battle to the strong, neither yet bread to the wise, nor yet riches to men of understanding, nor yet favor to men of skill: but time and chance happeneth to them all."

ORWELL'S VERSION:

Objective consideration of contemporary phenomena compels the conclusion that success or failure in competitive activities exhibits no tendency to be commensurate with innate capacity, but that considerable element of the unpredictable must invariably be taken into account."

After rendering these two examples of obfuscation and logorrhea, he noted that excluding the words objective, contemporary, and invariably could be eliminated without compromising the meaning of the blurb.

The intent here should not be taken as a lesson in sentence structure and content, but rather an example of how language can be polluted by verbal sewage.

WHAT GOOD IS RELIGION?

R eligion has been defined as, "A people's belief and their opinions concerning the existence, nature, and worship of a deity or deities, and divine involvement in the universe and human life." Such a comprehensive definition captures the essence of how the human mind deals with the unknown. *Homo sapiens* have always had an active imagination and an insatiable curiosity. Whenever they were unable to discover an acceptable explanation for something, they simply invented one. Religion is such an invention.

It is difficult to find a culture on this planet in which people live in perfect harmony. The only place that comes to mind is the fictitious Shangri la in the 1937 film called, Lost Horizon. In it, differences were respected and a climate of love characterized everyday life. While there may well be pockets of this fantasy in our world, television and computers will soon change all that. It will provide people in every country with an opportunity to see how others live. This will dramatically illustrate differences.

Every religion consists of a specific mind-set and its followers are expected to embrace that world view. Apostates run the risk of ex-communication.

Critical thinking and religious dogma are incompatible. This constitutes one of religion's greatest weaknesses. Thinking outside the box is unacceptable. While there are some that encourage honest and well-intended inquiry, they are rare.

Organized religions, from their inception, succeeded because humans are endowed with the ability to think in the abstract; they talk about things that do not materially exist as if they did. This is called reification. Terms like God, heaven, hell, shame, guilt, and sin are prime examples. In most religions, it is their stock and trade. In fact, most religions would cease to exist if such terms were excised from their liturgy.

Another negative aspect of organized religion is the element of control. In biblical times, those guilty of adultery were stoned, heretics were burned at the stake, infidels were crucified. Unconditional obedience was and still is the *sine qua non* of religion. Congregates must exhibit total obedience and humbly submit to a religion's ritualistic demands.

Let us now turn to the upside of religion; what is good about it? Its most valuable contribution to humanity is hope. Life, for most of us, is a roller coaster. Managing the good times seldom presents a problem. Managing the bad times such as sickness, death, divorce, and poverty all require inner strength, courage, and perseverance. Religion has always provided its followers with an open door, a safety net for those who feel abandoned and hopeless.

Another good thing about religion is its ability to make people feel connected, give them a sense of community, of togetherness. People enjoy an inner peace when they worship together. When they feel that all is lost and there is no point to go on living, the clergy stands with open arms to render support and sincere commiseration.

It is counter-productive to speak of religion as being either good or bad. It is like trying to decide whether a gun is good or bad. It depends upon how it is used and for what purpose. Religions do not exist in a vacuum, but in a cultural context. Each religion should be judged by how it applies the tenets upon which it is based from a strictly behavioral perspective. Actions definitely speak louder than words.

What would the world be like without religion? Pessimists argue that there would be complete anarchy. The Old and New Testament speak of original sin and cite the Adam and Eve myth in the Garden of Eden. If one starts with such a negative view of humanity, it bodes well for a self-fulfilling prophecy to emerge. If, however, one were to invest humanity with innate goodness, there might not be a need for religion.

Do people actually need to be threatened by a religious anathema in order for them to be morally and ethically good?

There comes a time in everyone's life when the impractical becomes practical, the unreasonable becomes reasonable, the unimaginable become imaginable, and the unreal becomes real. Religions address these phenomena by offering answers. Whether the answers are right or wrong, good or bad, rational or irrational, logical or illogical, will always depend upon whether they fulfill a felt need without hurting others and serve the greater good.

DIAGNOSIS vs TREATMENT

I n the medical profession, profits earned from diagnosis far exceed those from treatment. In the media, ads and editorials urge people to be tested for everything from syphilis to cirrhosis of the liver. Practically every other television commercial frightens viewers into believing they might have some mysteriously undiagnosed disease. They list a battery of symptoms that send up red flags. To support the claims made for their products, questionable studies are cited that are funded by pharmaceutical companies.

On the street and behind closed doors, drugs are illegally bought and sold by drug-pushers and addicts. Ironically, drug companies do the same thing with impunity. Early in the 20th century, snake-oil peddlers toured the country touting phony substances alleged to cure everything from baldness to ingrown toenails. The analogy is not without merit.

Drug companies employ field representatives who visit physicians offering generous perks designed to encourage them to purchase and use of their product. Using hindsight, could these drug reps be called, "drug pushers?"

Physicians who overtest their patients are never faulted. It is only when they fail to order a test deemed a medical necessity that they are held responsible. Hence, to avoid a malpractice suit, doctors often prescribe extremely expensive and needless diagnostic tests. The cost of an average MRI can range between $400 to $3,500 depending upon which MRI procedure is performed and where it is performed.

In 2010, echocardiograms accounted for more than $1.1 billion dollars; approximately eleven percent of total Medicare imaging. In 2014, the cost was exponentially higher. When the cost of all these diagnostic tests are weighed against the cost of all the treatments associated with their them, the costs are even higher.

The initial visit of a new patient to a physician's office usually begins with the establishment of a diagnosis, not with the immediate prescription of a medication. The alarm bell in contemporary medicine extols the importance of diagnosis, rather than treatment. While both play a critical role in the pursuit of wellness, without a viable diagnosis, all else is meaningless.

The term "corporate medicine" has recently become the hallmark of healthcare in America. It has become distressingly common for HMOs and other medical enterprises to have business-school trained managers putting factory-style production parameters on doctor visits. Doctors who spend too much time with their patients are considered disruptive and accused of breaking corporate management's precious guidelines.

Corporate medicine's approach to healthcare regards diagnosis as is its Golden Goose. It preempts all other medical procedures and is the most profitable.

FORGIVENESS

T o forgive someone of wrongdoing is, in a sense, to condone it. In Christianity, the confessional is a example of forgiveness at work. Individuals can commit practically any form of wrongdoing and, by simply confessing or showing remorse, be absolved of any guilt, shame, or blame. One wonders whether such a convenient method of absolution actually discourages future transgressions.

In terms of how severe a sentence our courts impose on a criminal, they display a measure of forgiveness if the criminal shows genuine remorse. While it does not excuse the crime, it takes repentance into consideration.

If a close look is taken at forgiveness, there is a difference between the person doing the forgiving and the one being forgiven? Research has shown that active forgiveness produces a number of valuable health benefits. It improves cardiovascular function, reduces chronic pain, lowers blood pressure, relieves depression, enhances immunity, and creates an elevated level of self-worth. Those who forgive also have their faith in human kindness and compassion confirmed.

Forgiveness is widely misunderstood. It is not simply saying, "That's O.K.," but a process that allows the victim to vent intense emotional pain and replace it with inner resolution and peace. It is a constructive gesture that breaks apart cycles of violence and vengeance by offering a prospect of hope for the future. You can forgive the person without forgiving the act.

Look at those who are forgiven. Will being forgiven cause perpetrators to refrain from committing similar crimes in the future? Does forgiving condone what they did? Should the Japanese be forgiven for attacking Pearl Harbor? Should America be forgiven for dropping the atom bomb on Nagasaki and Hiroshima? Should Adolph Hitler be forgiven for exterminating millions of Jews? Is there anything that is unforgiveable?

People unwilling to forgive the perpetrators of these heinous crimes have their reasons; e.g., They do not deserve forgiveness, that forgiveness is a sign of weakness, that being forgiven will not discourage them from committing future inhuman acts, and that revenge provides greater personal satisfaction.

Developing the ability to forgive keeps small disappointments from developing into big ones. It is not a skill that can be learned like driving a car or operating a computer. We all have the inherent ability to forgive. Forgiving someone does not mean you have to accept them back into your life. Forgiveness is giving up any hope that the past could have turned out differently. The uplifting reward goes to the forgiver, not to the forgiven.

Individuals who persist in faulting someone who said or did something to them many years ago significantly increase the unpleasantness of the experience. In time, it takes a terrible toll on their physical and emotional sense of well-being. A choice has to be made. Not forgive and stay stuck, or forgive and move on. Since it is impossible to be resentful and satisfied at the same time, forgiveness is the best way to eliminate the desire for revenge.

THE VALUE OF HERESY

W hile the word heresy usually applies to those in religion whose ideas clash with accepted orthodox opinion, it can be used to describe anyone who thinks outside of the proverbial box.

For millennia, historians have given little or no credit to heretics. If voices such as Jesus, Gallileo, Darwin and Einstein had fallen upon deaf ears, the pages of history might have taken a serious change in shape and direction. Their attitudes, values, and beliefs prompted those having a different point of view to be labeled heretics, quacks, or impostors.

For millennia, societies have resisted a departure from the *status quo*. People tend to perceive things the way they are as a security blanket, a safety net. A compelling example occurred in 1925 in Dayton, Tennessee. It involved a biology teacher named John Scopes who was accused of violating the Tennessee Butler Act that made it unlawful to teach evolution in its schools. Pejoratively called the, "Monkey Trial," it attracted worldwide attention and referred to Scopes as a heretic.

The pages of history contain countless examples of instances in which individuals were singled out and charged with heresy. The non-violent punishment meted out ranged from public disgrace, being shunned, ostracized, and humiliated. More severe punishment consisted of being imprisoned, exiled, excommunicated, tortured, or killed.

Once ideas become an endangered species, our civilization is on a collision course.

Schools and parents should encourage the younger generation to entertain popular and unpopular ideas with equal respect; with an open and unbiased mind. A future heretical voice may provide the key to our global survival.

Helen Keller believed that the heresy of today becomes the orthodoxy of tomorrow. Thomas Paine contended that the pen was mightier than the sword when he wrote: "Progress is born of doubt and inquiry. The Church never doubts, never inquires. To doubt is heresy, to inquire is to admit that you do not know—the Church does neither."

KNOWLEDGE ALONE IS NOT WISDOM

T hose under the age of twenty-one are seldom interested in wisdom. While exceptions exist, they are rare. Wisdom is shaped by a wide range of experience and the ability to see relationships; i.e., the big picture..

Unschooled people can acquire wisdom. Simply stated, wisdom is an awareness of wholeness that does not lose sight of the particular or the concrete. According to Socrates, the only true wisdom is knowing that you know nothing.

Any discussion of wisdom must be approached holistically, rather than on an insular basis. There is no magic bullet that automatically guarantees someone wisdom. A popular misconception is that intelligent people are automatically considered to be wise. That is not true. Intelligence should only be viewed as the means by which a motivated individual can accumulate wisdom.

Ironically, wisdom is in short supply among contemporary world leaders. The current political unrest in many parts of the world bespeaks this lack of wisdom at the top. If it does exist, it is cleverly disguised.

A prime example of wisdom is the Talmud, a collection of Rabbinic writings created to act as a guidebook for life. It contains everything from how to raise children, grow crops, heal the sick, and run a business.

People who are wise see the big picture -- the way things relate to one another and how that relationship plays out in everyday life. Individuals with an inability to recognize that all things are directly or indirectly connected tend to live a cocoon, a one-size fits all existence. Those who know that they do not know possess wisdom. Those who think they know, but are not aware that they do not know, lack wisdom.

The downside of wisdom is that it may not always lead to a solution. In seeing the big picture, it often neglects including ways of correcting a problem. Consider the field of medicine. There are physicians and researchers who possess a thorough and in-depth knowledge of a particular disease, but are unable to come up with a cure. There appears to be a marked difference between knowing and doing.

Copthorne MacDonald, in his book, Matters of Consequence, presents a variation on the concept of wisdom. To him, it entails a high level of relevancy, an intellectual understanding derived from science, the humanities, and economics. It should then be integrated with a sophisticated sense of self-awareness.

Wisdom does not exist in a vacuum, but is a context. When a wise person is confronted by a completely new situation, one with which he is unfamiliar, he should approach it logically and holistically. Although the wise individual would probably make a reliable appraisal of the situation, and propose a viable solution, there is always an element of risk; i.e. Murphy's Law: "If anything can go wrong, it will go wrong." Wisdom is the key to the good life, the joy of living. It nourishes the brain and warms the heart.

UNDERBELLY OF PERSPECTIVE?

In this treacherous world,
nothing is the truth or a lie.
Everything depends upon
the color of the crystal
through which one sees it.

Calderón de la Barca

There are two kinds of perception: biologic and psychologic. Biologic perception refers to information coming to us from our five senses. Psychologic perception relates to information from our mind. Most perspectives consist of a mixture that the brain then choreographs into meaningful units of thought.

Arthur Conan Doyle's fictitious Sherlock Holmes said, "Perspective is everything, details are nothing." While details are certainly important, they must be viewed in a context. A point of view invested with too many details is like getting all dressed up with no place to go.

A perspective does not exist in a vacuum. Imagine someone's perspective on education or politics. Imagine that their perspective zeros in on only one aspect of the subject. For example, a perspective on education focusing only on tenure is myopic. A step back must be taken from any perspective in order to see the big picture; i.e., time, place, and circumstance.

Another way of approaching a perspective is to consider what is referred to as a rival hypotheses --- an alternative way of viewing it by other credible individuals. We think differently about a perspective when we emotionally remove our self from a situation, rather than being directly immersed in it.

As we get closer to understanding a perspective, the abstract becomes more concrete. The most confusing aspect of a perspective is when it employs ambiguous terms such as good/bad, right/wrong, true/false, possible/impossible.

Perspectives can also be taken to be important or trivial, relevant or irrelevant, essential or superfluous. These considerations must be defined and clarified in any difference of opinion.

Imagine that your lover or spouse always brings you flowers on your birthday. One year, when he fails to do it, your perspective might suggest that he no longer loves you. However, remembering all the times he did bring flowers will dispel your inaccurate perspective.

A number of things can distort or compromise a perspective; e.g., stress, insomnia, forgetfulness, medication, or coercion by another person. Perceptions are not cast in stone. They are invested with the capacity to change by an aggressive application of willpower.

Perspective exemplifies intelligence, character and personality --- the way you view the world. If you want to get to know someone better, you must become familiar with their perspective on things. If you want to change yourself, you have to change your own perspective.

A number of things can distort a perspective; e.g., stress, insomnia, medication, distraction, memory lapse, or coercion by another person.

Perception involves selectivity. We choose what we prefer seeing, hearing, tasting, touching, smelling and doing. Any of these choices is capable of creating or modifying our self-image, self-worth, or self-esteem.

Sociological perspectives with which our government is currently struggling entail global warming, immigration, gay marriage, transgender surgery, racism, and weapons of mass destruction. Each of these issues involve perspectives on which solutions can produce a consensus among experts.

Overall, perception is a prismatic phenomenon which, if held up to the light of reason, tolerance, and open-mindedness, provides us with an antidote to the ills from which civilization suffers.

CONFRONTING THE IMPOSSIBLE

"It can't be done!" Throughout recordable history, those with an idea of doing something differently were inhibited by public opinion. Practically any form of progress would never have come to pass had those individuals been discouraged and prompted to abandon their endeavor. Caruso was told his voice sounded like a tin can, Edison was told that no one would listen to sound coming from a screen, Olivier was told to give up acting, Curie was told to forget about radium, Ford was told to stop trying to build a car that people would not buy. Had none of these people followed their dream, challenged the impossible, the world would have suffered great losses. Thomas Huxley put it best when he wrote, "Try to learn something about everything and everything about something."

The very notion of impossibility, the word itself, is a linguistic invention that can and should be eliminated from every language. Instead of serving a useful purpose, it acts as an unnecessary and obstructive agent.

Between the extremes of impossibility and certainty, there is possibility, plausibility, and probability. Each constitutes a portal of entry to the inventive mind, an avenue of opportunity. No civilization can survive or thrive by dispiriting creative minds.

In sports, limits have come and gone. In weight-lifting, in the forties and fifties of the 20th Century, someone who could clean and jerk 300 pounds was taken to be at the outer limits of the sport. By the end of that century, nearly 500 pounds was being hoisted aloft.

No matter what sport one chooses to examine, records continue to be broken. The figure skating of film star Sonia Heny in the thirties are currently looked upon as extremely simplistic. Back then, a triple or quadruple axel jump would have been considered impossible. Today, an increasing number of young skaters are doing triple axels as a matter of standard routine.

Another example of overcoming the impossible can be seen in hospital operating rooms in the form of heart and kidney transplants, quadruple cardiac bypasses, and a wide variety of other organs being moved from patient to patient. Surgeons, through the use of a heart-lung machine can now physically stop the heart and, while the patient is being supported on that miraculous machine, replace or repair heart valves.

In the 19th Century, the very idea of talking with someone thousands of miles away was deemed impossible. Today, through an invention called a cell phone, people communicate, instantly, with anyone, anytime, and anywhere. Space travel, likewise, has converted the impossible to the possible. A number of astronauts, today, can look up at the moon and say, "I was up there."

In the days of Columbus, it took months to sail cross the Atlantic. Today, thanks to the Wright brothers, we can fly to England in a matter of hours. Equally unimaginable is cloning;, taking a single cell from one person and, like a copying machine, make an exact duplicate.

The only area in which the word impossible now poses a real threat falls under the heading of weapons of mass destruction. Our inventiveness has brought us to the end of the road. Why? Because we now have at our disposal an instrument capable of destroying our entire planet and everything on it.

Having posed this extremely pessimistic view of tomorrow, there may well be scientists on Earth who refuse to accept such a negative outcome and, by so doing, courageously confront the impossible with confidence and purpose.

Let me close this discussion of confronting the impossible with mention of the computer. Children these days can sit at their computer and, with the click of a tiny finger, gain access to an unlimited and virtually inexhaustible body of information. Yesterday's science fiction has become today's science. It is mind-boggling to think of how people living in the year 2500 A.D. will talk about the today's technology. They will probably regard our technology in very much the same way we now perceive the life style of the caveman.

Printed in the United States
By Bookmasters